# BEER SOMMELIER

A JOURNEY THROUGH THE CULTURE OF BEER

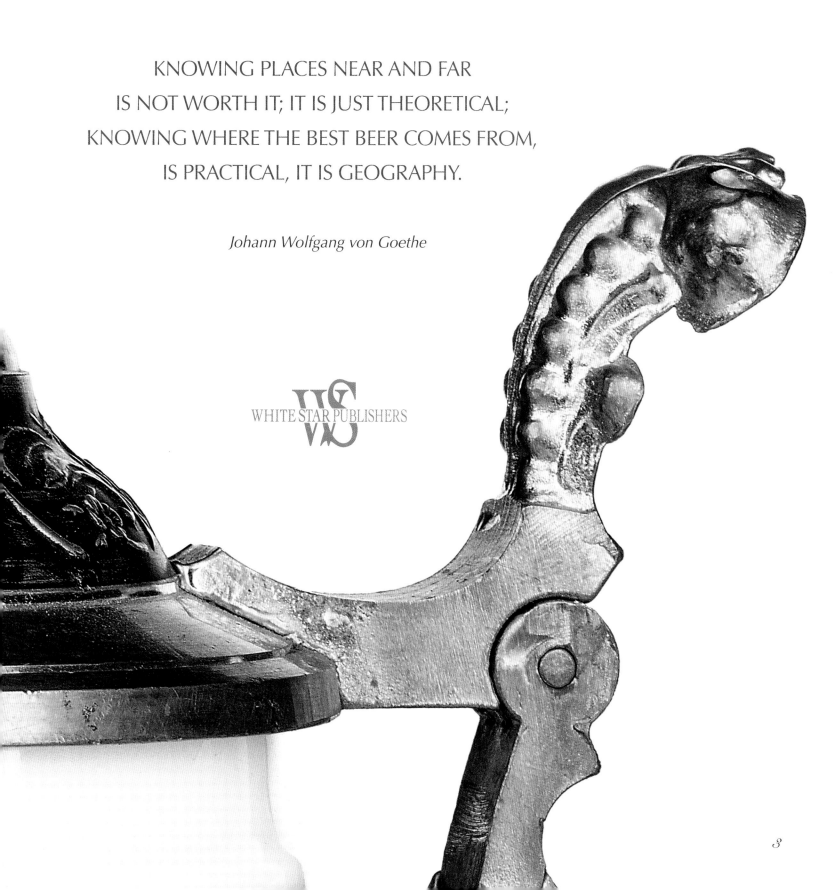

KNOWING PLACES NEAR AND FAR
IS NOT WORTH IT; IT IS JUST THEORETICAL;
KNOWING WHERE THE BEST BEER COMES FROM,
IS PRACTICAL, IT IS GEOGRAPHY.

*Johann Wolfgang von Goethe*

WHITE STAR PUBLISHERS

Project editor  VALERIA MANFERTO DE FABIANIS

Editorial assistant  LAURA ACCOMAZZO

Graphic design  MARIA CUCCHI

PHOTOGRAPHS BY FABIO PETRONI

TEXT BY PIETRO FONTANA

RECIPES BY CHEF GIOVANNI RUGGIERI

# CONTENTS

# PREFACE

Beer, which is now becoming a fashion phenomenon, is the is oldest and most widespread fermented product in the world.

Today we hear about it everywhere, from the United States to Australia and Japan, and of course throughout Europe. People are asking for craft beers in pubs, they are talking about micro-breweries, and they are enjoying beers that have amazing, original flavors and remarkable aromas.

It is a new phenomenon that has a twin character: that of innovation and tradition. The first originated in the United States in the late 1970s, while the second came from Great Britain, where the enthusiasts of CAMRA (the Campaign for Real Ale) are committed to recovering the Anglo-Saxon tradition that had gone missing.

Micro-breweries had been spreading in the United States since the 1970s and in the late 1990s small groups of pioneers elsewhere began producing beers. New breweries opened in Belgium next to the existing ones; Scandinavia and Denmark gave further impetus to micro-breweries, Italy began producing artisanal beers and the Czech Republic, liberated from the Iron Curtain, contributed to renewing its traditions. So the movement spread throughout the world, from north to south, from east to west.

Of course such beers have always existed, but they were taken for granted and dropped into oblivion, leaving only commercial lagers that were always very similar with bland colors and flavors. Without demonizing these consumer products, it is worth remembering that beer is a living product, able to stimulate the senses and to tell a story, that of the brewer with his pitcher and of the land where he grew up and works, and to do this, all that is needed it to learn to "listen."

This book is a first step in a journey to becoming knowledgable about the brewing world.

I hope that for you Gambrinus's passion for drinking will be like a vision on the road to Damascus. Never forget that beer is the third (or fourth, or fifth…) friend at the table when you are chatting, perhaps in a pub in the evening, and that it knows how to stand on the sidelines without being irritating, while giving great satisfaction with every sip and, if not drunk to excess, it will also help the conversation flow.

Cheers!

*Andrea Camaschella*

This 16th-century engraving of the English school shows the hop harvest. The female flowers of this sun-loving
climber are typically collected in late summer. They are used to give beer its characteristic bitter taste,
and a multitude of different aromas (spicy, herbaceous, fruity, citrus and resinous).

# THE ORIGINS OF BEER

## BEER B.C.

It is not possible to establish exactly when beer first came into being. What we do know is that since humans started practicing agriculture and building settlements where they lived while waiting to harvest cereals, beer has been made. Finds dating from 8000 B.C. in Palestine and Jordan, in the regions of Jericho, Nahal Oren and Tell Aswad, have revealed the first "semi-domesticated" grains, selected by farmers and different from the wild forms. Certainly some of them or some like them will have been used in the first, probably fortuitous, preparations of beer in the history of humanity.

The processes of fermentation were discovered independently and over thousands of years in many regions of the planet: from North America to Mesopotamia, from South America to Africa there is evidence of traditional foods made from a watery cereal broth that was left to ferment. With the invention of writing, the first written reference to beer, dating from around 4000 B.C., was made by the Sumerians in Mesopotamia: tablets and bas-reliefs tell of a drink prepared with barley, cooked bread and water called "kas," meaning "that which the mouth desires." This drink, usually prepared by the women and flavored with dates or honey, was drunk from large communal vessels, from which people drank together using long straws, such as have been found among the funereal objects in the royal cemetery of Ur. The beer of the Sumerians formed part of the wages of many workers; it was also sacred to the goddess Ninkasi and it was mentioned in the hymns addressed to her. Since its first appearance in the written history of humanity, beer has been considered a precious commodity as well as a way of creating conviviality among people. In the next Mesopotamian civilization, that of the Babylonians, there are numerous indications of the existence of beer in their daily life: the first written body of laws in history, the code of Hammurabi, already included laws concerning beer! In particular the code stipulated that beer should be distributed on a daily basis to the inhabitants in quantities varying according to their class. Anyone who commercialized it without authorization or watered it down was punished with death. Subsequent discoveries reveal that about twenty different types of beer (from the pale ones called "liquid bread" to flavored dark ones) were sold in Babylonian markets, and also that they were traditionally part of the offerings to celebrate the deceased during funeral rituals, where again everyone drank beer together. In ancient Egypt beer was considered a national drink: diluted with water and honey, it was even given to babies while they were being weaned or when the mother did not have enough milk. There are also numerous papyri containing preparations and medicinal recipes based on beer: in the famous Ebers Papyrus alone there are over six hundred! Beer was seen as a real food and, for instance, it formed an important part of the meals given to the men working on building the pyramids. This was a version with a high alcohol content, produced on a vast scale from malt and flavoring ingredients such as hop, juniper, ginger and so on. During the reign of the Pharaoh Ramesses II the production of beer was regulated and the scribes introduced a new hieroglyph to represent a craft that would flourish throughout the centuries: that of master brewer.

In the sacred Hebrew texts, the Bible and the Talmud, beer is mentioned several times and is the drink taken during the Feast of Unleavened Bread that recalls the flight from Egypt and during the Feast of Purim. In ancient Greece beer was drunk mainly during the celebrations in honor of Demeter, the goddess of the harvest and grain, as well as during the Olympiads when the consumption of wine was forbidden. On the Italian peninsula, before the Romans, the Etruscans were already drinking "pevakh," a drink originally made from spelt and rye, later from wheat, and again flavored with honey. According to Celtic tradition, the hero Mag Meld was able to found the Irish nation thanks to the strength he derived from beer whose recipe he had stolen from the mythological wood-dwelling Fomorians. In the Germanic civilization the first historical evidence linked to beer goes back to 800 B.C., the date of a beer amphora discovered near Kulmbach.

The citizens of Rome, more inclined to drink wine, also started to drink beer especially after encountering the Gauls and Germanic tribes. Indeed it was beer rather than wine that was produced in all the regions inhabited by the Celtic and Germanic tribes because vines did not grow well in the colder climate of Northern Europe, although they do now because of climate change. When Gnaeus Julius Agricola, governor of Britain, returned to Rome after his military campaigns, he brought back with him three master brewers from Glevum (present-day Gloucester) so that he could brew for himself and the more adventurous Romans the drink that he had learnt to appreciate in all the years he had spent abroad!

## BEER A.D.

In the first centuries A.D., Imperial Rome knew and appreciated beer but always as an "exotic" product: there is evidence that Nero received gifts of beer from the Iberian peninsula and that he had a Portuguese slave at his court whose only job was to produce beer for the emperor. In his Naturalis Historia Pliny described and catalogued the two great types of beer known in the empire: "zythum," of Egyptian origin, and "cerevisia," from Gaul and the Celtic regions. The great historian and naturalist wrote about the widespread propagation of this drink in the imperial provinces. In the capital of the Roman Empire beer was known but not very widely consumed; instead it was used by women in cosmetics, for instance for cleaning the face or nourishing the skin.

With the ever-increasing numbers of Germanic tribes settling within the confines of the empire, before its fall, obviously beer also became more widespread. These tribes also brought their traditions with them, such as the gruit tax, a form of taxation based on the quantity of beer produced. At that time in history beer was still made with fermented cereals but with the additions of aromas such as herbs, roots and berries of all kinds; some of these were dangerous, causing hallucinogenic effects or even lethal poisoning.

In the meantime, with the spread of Christianity the monasteries soon became points of reference for rural populations as far as food supplies and the production of food and drink, including beer, were concerned.

*This miniature from the* Treatise of Medicine *by Hildebrand of Florence (1356) shows beer being made from barley and other cereals. In the brewhouse are the vats of water and cereal being mashed, stirred continuously by the brewnmaster..*

In fact monasteries, abbeys and later castles set up and perfected the production of beer in enormous quantities, with significant effects on everyday life.

But above all, although they did not know it, by drinking beer people avoided the diseases and poisoning that were the norm among those who drank water, since that was often contaminated and unhealthy.

Also, during periods of monastic fasting, drinking beer was permitted and so this "liquid bread" was consumed as food. As result, the rules of the various monastic orders allowed the monks to drink large quantities of beer. The Venerable Bede stipulated the precise quantity of beer to be consumed at each meal while participants at the council of Aquis Grana were allocated four liters each a day, in other cases five liters, and there are reports of monasteries with limits of seven liters a day!

According to the rigid rule of the order founded by the Irish Saint Columba, beer was replaced by water as a severe punishment. Among the stories surrounding Saint Columba, there is one that tells how with a mere puff the saint exploded a vat of beer that pagans were sacrificing to Odin. He then scolded them for wasting beer by giving it to the devil and invited them to get some more, which he then blessed before handing it around: beer is a blessing of God but only if it is drunk in his name.

The queen of the Lombards Teodolinda, who established her court in Italy at Monza where she died in 627, was one of the first to convert the Germanic tribes to Catholicism. She was in regular correspondence with Pope Gregory the Great to whom she sent a very precious gift: a large quantity of beer that the Pope, perhaps because of Rome's historic preference for wine, gave away to the poor and to pilgrims: once again beer was the "liquid bread" that fed the travelers!

The first monastic brewery mentioned in written documents was that of the abbey of Weihehstephan, built in 724. In all monasteries it was the custom to divide the wort based on quality: the "prima" or "melior" was the beer reserved for consumption during feast days prescribed by the Church, the "secunda" was to be drunk on festive occasions and on Sundays, while the "tertia" was for daily consumption, always as "liquid bread." It was also offered to travelers and pilgrims who visited the monasteries and stayed there.

In the monasteries the production of beer began to be regulated and standardized in 1067 when Hildegard of Bingen, botanist and abbess of the German monastery of Saint Rupert, experimented with the use of hops as flavoring. According to historical documents, this plant, known to monastic herbalists for its calming and anti-bacterial effects, was used in the production of beer for the first time shortly after Charlemagne's coronation in 800. But it was mostly used for its calming and disinfecting properties during childbirth. Hildegard had the idea of using hops instead of the herbs used normally in the gruit. These herbs, because of their uncontrollable effects (including, as mentioned above, hallucinations and even fatal poisoning), were now recognized as dangerous and the authorities even discussed the possibility of forbidding the production of beer completely. Some people also claimed that "witch hunts" were connected with the production of beer, remarking on the strange and mysterious deaths of people who, having drunk beer prepared with strange concoctions by women, behaved crazily and as if possessed by the devil.

It was also for this reason that gradually, besides home-made beer and that produced in monasteries and by the aristocracy (in abbeys, monasteries and castles), beer came to be made under public control. In the Anglo-Saxon world this led to the creation of public places where the locals could drink beer produced in a way that could be trusted. These were known as "Public Houses," a name quickly abbreviated to "pub," a word that still today throughout the world describes a place where you can drink beer!

Beer as a healthy drink (because of the way it is made), unlike water that often came from swamps or polluted wells, is also mentioned in the stories of Saint Arnold, today the patron saint of Belgian beer. It is said that in the 15th century he saved the inhabitants of Soissons from a cholera epidemic because he had noticed that people who drank beer were less prone to catching the disease than those who drank water. So he invited all the population to drink beer that he had stirred with his pastoral staff and blessed himself.

In any case, after Hildegard of Bingen's experiments hop-based beer soon spread all over Europe through trade and contacts with the cities of the Hanseatic League—but not immediately to Great Britain where the production of local ales continued for a long time in public houses to the exclusion of continental beers made with hops. But as well as improving the taste of beer, the antiseptic properties of hops also made it more stable so that it would keep longer, so with this added advantage it eventually overcame the "competition" of other flavor enhancers.

The German Beer Purity Law, or Reinheitsgebot, was decreed on April 13, 1516, by William IV of Bavaria and it stipulated that beer could only be produced from water, barley malt and hops. So what about the yeast? At that time the existence of the micro-organism responsible for beer's fermentation was not yet known so it was not until the industrial revolution that this ingredient was also included in the Purity Law.

It is said that this edict was originally intended to remain in force for only one year, as a drastic solution to a terrible famine. Besides water and hops, brewers were only allowed to use barley malt to make beer in order to preserve the other cereals, particularly wheat, for "solid food."

In fact the Purity Law remained in force for much longer and in 1871 Bavaria agreed to become part of the German Empire on condition that the other states adhered to it. More recently, the European Union demanded that this law be suspended in Germany to allow the free circulation of beer produced in other States. But in fact most brewers still adhere to it as far as the ingredients are concerned, since wheat has subsequently been accepted as ingredient and (once it had been discovered) yeast was included. This law also used to regulate the periods of production and sale.

# INDUSTRIAL BEER

About a hundred years after the Purity Law was passed and beer had crossed the Atlantic Ocean to arrive in North America with the Pilgrim Fathers on board the Mayflower, research and scientific discoveries took place that changed the production and consumption of beer forever.

The experiments made by Antonie van Leeuwenhoek with his improved microscope led to the discovery of the existence of yeast, identifying it as the key ingredient in beer production although it was not stipulated in the Purity Law. This defined three different traditions in Europe, three different ways of producing beer: the German/Bohemian, the Belgian and the Anglo-Saxon. But there now followed a period of great turbulence, endless wars and serious economic crises: beer was subjected to heavy taxes.

In the Anglo-Saxon world beer was still used as part of the workers' pay, at the end of a hard day's work; for instance English porters had their "porter" beer, produced by mixing two different qualities and served in pint glasses filled to the brim. In this case foam was not considered a good thing because it would have diminished the quantity of beer received in lieu of payment.

In Belgium the tradition of small brewers, starting with the brewing monasteries, continued to endure and the concept of local beer-making remained deep-rooted, while in the German/Bohemian world brewers experimented with large-scale beer-production. Although following different approaches, before the French Revolution all three traditions began experimenting with more innovative production systems, using the new instruments that the many scientific discoveries of the 18th century had made available: for instance, the thermometer, invented by Fahrenheit in 1760 and the densitometer that Marin made available in 1770.

In addition to these two inventions there was another that would change not only beer-making but also the whole world itself. In 1765 James Watt invented the steam engine that paved the way for "steam-brewing," speeding up production and increasing it.

There were ever more innovations. In the early 19th century Daniel Wheeler developed a modern malt toaster, while in the later years of the century Carl von Linde invented the refrigerator, enabling beer to be made 365 days a year. Previously it had been impossible to produce good beer in the spring and summer because of the higher temperatures and as a result production stopped in March. It was only resumed in September when weather conditions had cooled down, coinciding with the new hop harvest.

Refrigeration improved the preservation of the product while also leading to the development of the technique of "bottom fermentation" at a temperature of below 53 °F (12 °C), with a long period of maturation at a low temperature. The great protagonist of this technique was Christian Hansen who experimented with yeast while working in the Carlsberg laboratories: he succeeded in isolating a single yeast cell and reproducing it. What had until then been the most mysterious ingredient in beer-making was now completely under the control of the brewer. It was now possible to identify, isolate and reproduce the various types of yeast, using them in a specific manner for different beers, and to continue producing them with the same flavors and characteristics.

*This engraving from a book of the 17th century shows the hard work behind the scenes in an old brewery, at a time when barrels were completely dominant.*

Der Durst nach Sachen dieser Zeit
erwartet bittre Süssigkeit:
Such, Seele, deinen Durst zu laben
im Brunnen der von Segen fliest,
und gegen Arme sich ergiest
die um den Glauben Alles haben.

Louis Pasteur fine-tuned his pasteurization method so as to ensure the absence of infections or changes in beer. His method guaranteed a much longer period of preservation; this in turn gave the product a longer life and therefore a wider market and increased sales. Confirming the importance that the great scientist attached to his experiments with beer, one of his many books was one entitled "Studies on Fermentation," published in 1876.

Beer in barrels, warm, flat and dark-colored, produced on a small scale by a very large number of brewers distributed evenly across the land, using a potpourri of almost random yeasts, served in wooden or earthenware containers, had now become a romantic reminder of days gone by, definitively a thing of the past.

Industrial beer was light in color, fresh, sparkling, served in elegant glasses, and it was produced on an ever larger scale by ever more high-tech brewers. Beer was beginning to be distributed in barrels and in glass bottles with hermetic seals, so that the carbonation produced by the yeast remained intact until consumption, manifesting itself both in the effervescence and the foam. This was the triumph of modern beer!

In the 20th century the history of beer became intertwined with the complicated history of the period with its revolutions, world wars and prohibition. After the World Wars and reconstruction that followed, the world was ready for mass production: industrial beer in bottles, in cans and in barrels became ever more widespread, gradually wiping out the thousands of smaller artisanal breweries that had cropped up over the centuries, while large companies developed increasingly widespread distribution and marketing network, thus turning beer into a global product.

## THE RENAISSANCE OF BEER

The West experienced an economic boom in the 1960s and 1970s, enhanced by a feeling of well-being after the dark parenthesis of the two World Wars. This period was also marked by amazing changes in fashion, in ways of interacting with people, in ways of having fun and of enjoying leisure time, and beer too played a part in these. This was the era of music festivals and youth conventions, but above all it was marked by a new development, namely an interest in local products, products of quality that told the story of the places and the people involved in its creation. From being a "liquid food," beer had become a drink consumed for pleasure in its own right, and it was about to undergo another revolution, especially in Britain and the United States.

CAMRA (CAMpaign for Real Ale) was founded in England in 1971—the year I was born! It is an association that is still very active today with over 150,000 members throughout the world and it is the promoter of the legendary Great British Beer Festival (GBBF), an annual event that no beer enthusiast should miss. The term "Real Ale" was coined to highlight the distinction between the standard beers produced on a large scale by mega-groups and the "traditional" beers that were threatened with extinction, produced in various styles by small brewers using natural processes and methods. These always undergo secondary fermentation and they are matured in the barrels from which they are served directly in pubs, preferably using the "hand pump" or "pouring," two methods of serving beer that do not use gas to force the beer out of the barrel.

Thanks to CAMRA people have again become interested in rediscovering and appreciating traditional styles that are slowly reconquering a small but ever-growing number of beer drinkers and enthusiasts.

In the United States too a whole network of small local breweries is cropping up everywhere, after being almost completely annihilated by large-scale industrial production and the global supremacy of the light-colored lagers, the taste, flavors and type of which are almost identical throughout the world.

As always the movement was triggered by the passion of a small group of various kinds of people. One such was the entrepreneur Fritz Maytag who bought the Anchor Brewing Company in 1965 and started adding some "special" beers to its standard production. He created the prototype of the "artisanal" brewery and "artisanal" beer.

Then ordinary people became interested in the idea of home-brewing, making their own beer at home, reviving a tradition that is very ancient, as mentioned above. Rather than being an affectation or a reaction against mass-production and growing consumerism, home-brewing was purely and simply a necessity: at that time it was impossible to find more than two or three different types of quality beers produced industrially in the United States; a simple visit to Belgium could convince the American beer enthusiast that enough was enough.

And it was a passionate home-brewer who wrote the next chapter. In 1976, driven by his passion for beer-making, he took a giant step and founded an artisanal brewery, The New Albion Brewery, in Sonoma, California. Before it closed a few years later he had inspired many others to imitate what he had done, bringing about a real revival in American brewing.

Thanks to the unflagging passion of people such as Charlie Papazian (president of the American Brewers Association and founder of the American Home-Brewers Association) and of small groups of enthusiasts, artisanal beer production became an ever-expanding phenomenon: the ten small brewers that had sprung up in the USA during the 1980s began to grow. Their number really began to explode between 1990 and 1995, with an increase in the number of small brewers and artisanal breweries that, having already increased by 35% in 1990 reached an incredible annual increase of 51% in the last year of that period. The sector is continuing to grow today at an interesting rate, and recent figures show how the over a thousand artisanal American brewers and brewpubs are now producing several million barrels, a small but significant percentage of the total amount of beer drunk in the United States.

This movement has also had an influence in Europe where countries traditionally involved in the production of beer have started to rediscover ancient traditions and reintroduce production methods, flavors and types of beer that had fallen into oblivion, such as white beers and beers flavored with fruit, to mention just two.

Today the home-brewing movement and artisanal beer production has also converted some countries to drinking beer that in the past had not been very interested. Italy for example had only six artisanal producers in 1996 but today it has almost caught up with Belgium, with over 600 breweries.

I believe that this tempestuous expansion, which also runs the risk of generating a feeling of excess, confusion and suspicion in the average beer-drinker, will be confronted sooner or later by some historical events that—as has happened in the past—will cause serious problems for all small breweries and that they will suffer much more than the great international groups.

But as long a the philosophy inspiring beer production is based on joy, passion, quality and professionalism… beer will be safe!

# WHAT IS BEER?

I like to think of beer as a beautiful thing, good, cheerful, exciting, sociable and nourishing. It is beautiful in its enormous variety of colors and shades that range from pale yellow to the deepest black through all the nuances of amber, red and brown. The foam too is lovely, exuberant or shy, more or less persistent, but always expressive! It can be a creamy monument that is almost solid or a fleeting surge that makes a brief appearance long enough for a quick salute before turning into beer again.

Its myriads of bubbles are beautiful, sometimes very small, sometimes larger, sometimes very white, sometimes the color of cappuccino.

Its perfumes and its aromas are infinite, reminding us that it is made from the produce of the soil and that it is the work of man: wild flowers, fruits of every kind, aromatic herbs, spices, honey and various smoked products. Then it may be sweet, bitter, sour and salty in various degrees and different orders.

It invites us to look at it with our eyes, to smell it with our nose, to taste it with our mouth; it also encourages us to listen with our ears when we open a bottle and then pour it into a glass. Some beers flow from the bottle as light as water while others are thick like oil. What they want is for us to understand their personality and how to appreciate them.

It can be drunk in the company of friends or with adventurous acquaintances of a single night, whom we have never seen before and will never see again. It is a pleasure to enjoy on festive occasions, to celebrate, or to drink every day with a meal, after work or in the evening. When times are hard and difficult beer helps us to unwind or to take time to think.

But beers must also be savored so that they delight the senses and reveal the joy of good things while appreciating the skill and hard work of the brewer who made it for us. It is a pleasure to spend time choosing the right glass for the each beer from the myriads available: angular or with persuasive curves, short and squat or tall and slender, antique or modern, baroque or minimalist. It is also fun to examine the labels, admiring the pictures, the logos and the information on them, and last but not least the beautiful bottles and their stoppers.

Although all you can do with it is drink it, beer is pure emotion!

But what is beer? The question may seem trivial but that is far from the case.

First, because "there is no such thing as beer but there are many beers," to quote the words of the Italian poet of beer who is my mentor, Lorenzo "Kuaska" Dabove.

We all have some idea of what the beers of our own time may be, but when one remembers that this drink is as old as humanity and that it has also developed independently in many different geographical regions, it is easy to understand how incredibly complex it must be so that it is impossible to define it unequivocally, reduced to a single concept.

Of course, beer is a drink. But originally it must have been more like a watery minestrone soup, based on cereals.

Of course, it is alcoholic because it is fermented, and one must therefore drink it with moderation. But today there are also non-alcoholic beers, a category that in spite of the name may contain a very small amount of alcohol, within the limits set by individual countries.

Of course, it is made of cereals: barley, wheat, rye, sorghum, millet... From the dawn of time and still today, cereals have been the staple food of human beings because they are easy to grow, they keep for a long time and they have a high nutritional value derived from the starches (and therefore the sugars) that they contain. But there are also fermented beverages made from potatoes, which also contain a lot of starch, but they are not cereals!

Of course, it is flavored. In the last few centuries hops have been the main flavoring agent but before that many kinds of other essences have been used.

Of course, it is water-based. But do not think of water as an adulterating element used to dilute it and water it down. While grapes contain a lot of water naturally so that they produce a sweet liquid when pressed, cereal grains contain no water so when they are "pressed" they will only produce flour! This is why water is a noble ingredient that plays a vital part in brewing.

In an attempt to give a general definition and leaving deeper analysis for later in this book, let us say that beer is the product of the alcoholic fermentation, achieved by yeasts, of a sugary must extracted from barley malt and other cereals, malted or unmalted, flavored with hops.

# THE RAW MATERIALS

## WATER

Water is the main ingredient of beer and it is therefore extremely important. But water that is perfect and ideal for every kind of beer does not exist; on the contrary, each beer requires a specific type of water, that is, one with a particular concentration of mineral salts, and a particular hardness and pH that will define its flavor and influence the various production stages. Water also plays a fundamental part in all the phases of sanitizing and cleaning the installation and therefore the quantity used in brewing is enormous. The challenge today is to contain this use of water within more sustainable limits.

The availability of water with specific characteristics in some areas has in the past led to the creation of some kinds of beer that exist only in those areas. For example the very soft water with very few mineral salts found in the region of Pils in Bohemia was the essential starting point for all the beers that still bear that name today. On the other hand, in Ireland the very hard water rich in mineral salts is the basis of the country's typical stouts. Today the modern technology used in water treatment makes it possible to manipulate its composition, based on the particular production requirements. It is therefore possible to make the same type of beer with the same characteristics, regardless of where it is produced.

## YEAST (AND FERMENTATION)

"The brewer makes the wort but the yeast makes the beer." This motto, so dear to brewers, reminds us that the real star of the production process is yeast, a microscopic unicellular organism that transforms the wort prepared by the brewer into beer. The scientific etymology describes this quite clearly: *Saccharomyces* reminds us that it is a fungus (*-myces*) of sugar (*saccharo-*).

The yeast cells can "eat" the sugars and "produce" ethyl alcohol and carbon dioxide in the completely natural and physiological process (albeit rather complex to explain in detail) that is known as alcoholic fermentation. A metaphor that may not be very elegant but that is good for explaining the metabolism of yeast is that of our everyday life: we eat and we drink and then we go to the bathroom! It is the same with the yeast in alcoholic fermentation: it eats the sugars and evacuates the alcohol and carbon dioxide.

The great difference is that the by-products of the yeast are not thrown away but are completely and skillfully recycled in our glasses!

We are therefore not looking at a manufacturing process that "uses" alcohol (in the way that herb-flavored bitters do, for instance) or that "uses" carbon dioxide (as sparkling drinks do, it being added subsequently). We are talking here of a procedure that "produces" both.

In fact, the yeast colonizes the wort by endlessly multiplying (through cell division) until there is no sugar left to consume; therefore the alcohol level of the beer depends on the quantity of sugar in the wort. Since the sugar is

derived from the starch in the cereals, the more cereals the brewer uses for the same amount of water, the higher the strength. In some countries this concept is incorrectly understood by the law, which uses the generic and ambiguous term "double malt" (in other words, a double quantity of barley malt) to define beers with a high level of sugar and a high degree of alcohol.

The enormous surplus of yeast cells produced during fermentation led to it being used in making bread, hence the term "brewer's yeast."

Yeast is also responsible for producing numerous aromas, called esters, that give beer its unmistakable character and personality.

There are many carefully selected types of yeast used in brewing but they can all be grouped into two large families:

– *Saccharomyces cerevisiae* (*cerevisiae* = of the beer) are also called "top-fermenting" yeasts. They work at a relatively high temperature, between about 60 and 80 °F (15 and 25 °C) and in the "highest" part of the fermentation vessel, that is, close to the surface where they form a thick foam. These yeasts are the basis of all "top-fermenting" beers, and these are known by the generic name "Ale."

– *Saccharomyces carlsbergensis* are called "bottom-fermenting" yeasts. They work at a lower temperature than

the previous ones, below 53 °F (12 °C), and in the lower part of the fermentation vessel, that is, close to the bottom. These yeasts were isolated in the second half of the 19th century in the laboratories of the well-known Danish brewery after which they were named, Carlsberg. They were also usually present in the beers of lower Germany where it was customary to mature beer in the cool temperature of caves. The beers produced with these yeasts are called "bottom-fermenting" beers, and these are known by the German generic name "Lager."

## BARLEY MALT AND OTHER CEREALS

After water, barley malt is quantitatively the most important ingredient in beer. The process that transforms barley into malt is "malting." While in the past malting took place in the brewery and was the first stage in the brewing process, today it is entrusted to the professionalism and skill of a "maltster" outside the brewery. He has the delicate and important task of preparing a real "palette" of colors, flavors and perfumes for the brewer from which he will select to create his recipes. The malts are the only raw material that determines the final color of the beer and they also play a large part in its aromas and flavors, often reminiscent to honey, caramel, biscuit and coffee.

But what is malting exactly? First, the grains of barley are macerated in water in order to trigger their germination; in this phase, the enzymes in the grains that will transform the reserves contained in the seed are activated, to make the germ sprout. It is precisely these precious enzymes that are the brewer's allies in the preparation of the wort. The next stage is to dry the germinated seed, immediately interrupting the growing of the germ and the rootlets. A grain that has been interrupted at a more or less advanced state of growth will have a different chemical composition; by drying the grains for longer or shorter times and at higher or lower temperatures, malts are obtained that differ in color, flavor and aroma, and they will produce different beers. In the production of any type of beer, four malt bases, rich in enzymes, are mainly used: Pils and Pale (lighter), Vienna and Munich (reddish-brown); then special malts (caramelized or toasted) are added to these, but in smaller quantities.

Barley malt is so widespread and famous that, although there are other cereals that can be used to make malt, such as wheat, oat, rye, spelt, "malt" usually means barley malt. In some beers tradition has led to the use of other cereals such as malted wheat for Weiss beers, unmalted wheat for the Blanches, or malted rye for Roggenbier and the modern Rye IPA.

## HOPS

Although introduced rather late in the production of beer, in the Middle Ages, the hop (*Humulus lupulus*) today plays the undisputed leading role in brewing. Its main feature is that it adds the characteristic bitter taste to beer. In also adds a very typical aroma that varies depending on the soil and the region in which it is cultivated. It has antiseptic and antioxidant properties and it therefore acts as a natural preservative. Thanks to the abundant use of hops in their preparation, India Pale Ales, produced in England since the 18th century and transported by ship to India, managed to reach their destination with all their characteristics intact.

The hop is a perennial climber that belongs to the same family as hemp and it grows spontaneously in cold to temperate climates (to be precise, between latitudes 35° and 55° in both hemispheres). It produces male and female flowers: only the latter, rich in lupulin, essential oils and resins, are used in making beer. The varieties available are very numerous, and as in the case of the grapes used to make wine, they have specific characteristics that help to define the profiles of different beers. There are aromatic hops: herbaceous or spicy, floral or resinous, fruity or balsamic; on the other hand there are also others with a very bitter yet agreeable flavor. Some new generation hops have managed to combine both characteristics extremely successfully.

In the variegated panorama of beer production, it is not unusual to discover many other distinctive ingredients such as honey, ginger, coffee, fruit (cherries, strawberries, raspberries, figs, chestnuts…), spices (spices of all kinds, star anise, cinnamon…) or roots (licorice, gentian). While some of these ingredients are part of local traditions, others are the result of experimentation and research by brewers who enjoy playing and discovering new juxtapositions, in some cases even ones that are a little risky.

# HOW BEER IS MADE

Brewing is an art as ancient as man, simple yet complex, and it is easy to understand that there is no single way of making beer. In this section we shall discover the main stages of the process of beer-making, leaving to later chapters on the styles of beer the specific production details of various beers that make them unique and distinctive. Returning to the concept that yeast plays the leading role in the preparation of beer, it is evident that the entire process is geared to satisfying all the requirements of this microorganism so that it can carry out in the best possible way its delicate and irreplaceable task: that of "eating" the simple sugars and "producing" ethyl alcohol, carbon dioxide and series of other compounds that give the beer its aromas and flavors.

The first thing a brewer must do is to know exactly what type of beer he wants to obtain, in terms of color, degree of alcohol, aroma, taste, and balance. Then, having decided on the type, he must prepare a good recipe, making a selection from the various raw materials to choose those that are most likely to produce the desired result.

Having made this most important choice, he can start working on the actual process of beer-making. This consist of two major cycles: the hot side (with its stages of mashing, wort separation, sparging of the spent grains, boiling and whirlpool, cooling and oxygenation), and the cold side (divisible into primary fermentation, secondary fermentation and maturation).

## THE HOT SIDE

The hot side takes place at high temperatures and in brewing jargon it is called "the brew." It is carried out in a brewhouse containing a more or less automated assembly of large containers equipped with agitators, tubes, pumps, thermometers and thermostats. Most of us picture them as the gleaming copper vats that have a place of honor in many breweries but in reality copper is banned today, replaced by stainless steel, which is healthier and more practical; copper now only has an aesthetic and decorative function as the outer coating of these vessels.

### MASHING

The objective of this phase is to obtain the sweet wort resulting from the conversion of the starch into sugars. The correct proportions of water and cereals are mixed together in the mash tun, resulting in a kind of soft porridge. The water can be treated to a greater or lesser extent but it must definitely be hot, not cold and not boiling, so as to allow the enzymes, released during the malting process, to break up of the starch. All the cereals (malted and un-malted) are coarsely ground with the dual aim of splitting the grain and at the same time leaving the outer husk that protects it (the glume) as intact as possible. By doing this, the floury part is transformed into a solution with the hot water and this activates the action of the enzymes already present in the malted grain. The husks on the other hand will play a fundamental part in the subsequent filtration.

There are various enzymes present in the malt and each one of them performs a particular task at a particular temperature, so the brewer can make one or other work more or less intensely by varying the temperature to obtain the characteristics mentioned in the recipe.

The most important enzymes are those responsible for saccharification. These are Alpha-amylase and Beta-amylase that completely break up the complex starch molecule, formed of long chains of complex sugars, and transform it into molecules of more simple sugars. Beta-amylase produces mostly maltose, a disaccharide formed of only two molecules of wholly fermentable glucose (completely digestible by the yeasts and therefore completely transformable into alcohol and carbon dioxide). Alpha-amylase produces maltodextrin, polysaccharides that have from 3 to 17 units of glucose joined together and which, not being metabolizable by the yeasts, will remain in the finished beer and give it body and sweetness.

The role of other enzymes such as the proteolytic enzymes is to break down the proteins that could make the finished beer cloudy.

When all the starch has been converted into sugars, after about an hour and a half, the temperature is increased to stop the enzymatic activity and make the mixture more fluid so as to facilitate the next phase, filtration.

## FILTRATION

The aim of this phase is to retrieve only the sweet liquid while eliminating all the solid matter resulting from the split grains of the cereal residue.

The mixture is transferred into another container called a filtration vat into which the wort is poured. The vat has a filtrating double bottom on which the heavier solid parts sink and settle. This creates a "filtration bed," a thick, soft, stratified intertwining of glumes, grains and flour that acts as a natural filter, allowing the precious sweet liquid to percolate through it but catching all the particulates, even the finest and most powdery particles. If the grains and in particular the glumes, have been milled too finely, this operation would not be possible and would compromise the entire production.

Meanwhile the sweet wort is slowly collected in a new vat in which it will be boiled.

## RINSING

The filtration bed is then rinsed with fresh hot water both to extract the sugars that may have remained trapped in the filtration bed and to reach the required amount of wort. It should be remembered that in the next phase of the brew process a large part of the wort will be "lost"through evaporation and, anticipating this, it is during the rinsing stage that this loss must be compensate for. The time needed for the filtration process, rinsing and the gathering all the wort into the boiling vat is about one hour and a half. The solid waste of this phase can be completely recycled as animal feed for bovines and pigs.

## BOILING AND THE WHIRLPOOL

It is finally in this phase that hops are introduced. The temperature of the wort is increased to 210 °F (100 °C) and it is boiled for one or at the most two hours to ensure that it is sterilized. Moreover, at this temperature the resins in the hop become isomerized and dissolve as a result, releasing their bitterness. Another process that occurs in

this phase is that all the other proteins coagulate so that the finished beer is even more limpid. Also, the boiling process expels some of the unwanted aromatic components , such as DMS (dimethyl sulfide). But this "expelling" also risks losing some of the "good" aromas of the hops, which is why these aromatics are added in the final minutes of the boiling phase or even after it finished. In some beers with a strong hop presence, at the end of the boiling process the wort is put through special containers full of hops to extract the maximum aroma. In other cases, brewers may use the dry-hopping technique, where the aromatic hop is added directly to the fermentation vat. There, thanks to much lower temperatures, it releases yet a different range of aromas and flavors.

By now the wort will have been "soiled" again by the hopping and the formation of protein coagulates, so before transferring it to the fermentation vat to be worked on by the voracious yeasts, it must be separated from the solid particulate. Using a pump or agitator, the wort is stirred so that it forms a small vortex. By centropetal force, this concentrates all the solid particles that must be separated into the middle of the vat. Through a hole in the outer perimeter, the brewer decants the cleaned wort into the fermenter.

At this point there are only a few operations left for the brewer to complete. The boiling wort must be cooled down to a temperature that is right for the yeast, otherwise it would die. This must be done in as short a time as possible to prevent attacks by the bacteria and wild yeasts that are much attracted by this sterile wort in which they too would find an excellent environment. During the cooling, which usually takes place with the aid of a lamellar heat exchanger or a "tube in tube" one, the wort is also oxygenated to give the yeast the right quantity of oxygen it needs to reproduce itself. After a hard day's work the "brew" is finished.

## FERMENTATION

The yeast, properly prepared, is inoculated into the wort at the right temperature and begins to carry out its task. It has many simple sugars to metabolize and transform into ethyl alcohol and carbon dioxide, but with much foresight, before concentrating on them, it immediately begins to absorb all the oxygen available that will help it multiply itself, producing new generations of daughter cells that will help it in its lengthy task. Only after this phase of apparent calm (latency) does the true alcoholic fermentation start.

### PRIMARY FERMENTATION

Yeast is a real chemical micro-laboratory in its own right, rational, highly organized and indefatigable, workingtwenty-four hours a day for as long as there is food. In the initial stages, when the maximum amount of simple sugars is available, its action is so fierce that it raises the temperature in the fermenter; for this reason it is necessary to keep it under control by means of a cooling system to prevent it from rising too much. In fact, there is a risk of a vicious cycle developing: the higher the temperature rises, the faster the yeast works, and the faster it works the more heat it produces. In these thermal stress conditions it is natural that the yeast should produce unpleasant, undesirable aromatic compounds and flavors that are capable of completely ruining the beer. Above a certain temperature the yeast would undoubtedly die, thus stopping the fermentation process.

On the other hand, at the right temperature the yeast is able to work perfectly, transforming all the more simple sugars (glucose and maltose) in about a week while producing its specific aromatic-gustative profile. At this point primary fermentation is complete.

## SECONDARY FERMENTATION

In this phase the fermentation process slows down considerably and the temperature of the beer goes down. Many yeast cells are now inactive and they slowly begin to settle on the bottom, taking with them many other particles, especially protein compounds, thus starting the process of clarification that will come to a close only later, during maturation.

But there are still many active yeast cells in the beer as well as residues of simple sugars. These include maltodextrin molecules that will all remain in the finished beer except for the maltotriose cells, the simplest, that consist of three single glucose molecules, a sugar that can be slowly metabolized by the yeast (although not by all strains) during the secondary fermentation. The length of the secondary fermentation varies enormously depending on the type of beer. For the simpler beers it is not even necessary, while in other very complex beers such as the English Barley Wines or the German Doppel Bock, it can require a lot of time.

## MATURATION

At the end of the fermentation process the beer must be cooled to a very low temperature, to 32 °F (0 °C), to encourage the natural precipitation of the yeast, to refine the organoleptic profile and to stabilize it. The yeast can also be removed in a quicker and more invasive manner by subjecting the beer to processes of filtration or centrifugation or by the addition of colloidal substances, but these do not accelerate maturation. Other special types such as the Lambic or other beers matured in barrels, can require a maturation period of up to several years.

At the end of the maturation period the beer is finally ready to be bottled or put in cans. Depending on the style and the choices made by the brewer, it is possible to bottle beers that are already carbonated, or to obtain effervescence by secondary fermentation in the bottle. In this case the beer is "flat" when bottled or canned but a small amount of sugar is added (and if necessary some yeast), which is enough to trigger a small secondary fermentation. Since the containers are hermetically sealed, the carbon dioxide so produced remains dissolved in the beer, giving it its characteristic perlage and foam.

When bottling, the big brewers usually pasteurize the finished beer to guarantee better conservation and stability, by making sure that any bacteria still present in the beer are eliminated. Naturally this also means that the yeast still in it will be killed as well. The beers produced in this way are certainly stable, but it is also true that sophisticated palates and noses may be slightly disappointed.

# SPONTANEOUS FERMENTATION

Beer is a discovery that is believed to be completely fortuitous, going back to the dawn of civilization when man became settled and started cultivating cereals. The first document in which beer is mentioned dates back to 3800 B.C. It is a tablet that contains a hymn to Sikuru (which in Sumerian is thought to mean "liquid bread"), discovered in Nineveh, in present-day Iraq. That is all that remains of those beers: at that time it was a food preparation that was produced without any monitoring instruments, in not particularly hygienic conditions, but above all, no one was aware of the existence of yeast.

But it should not be completely dismissed. Over the years beer-making evolved with the malting of cereal and the introduction of new techniques. Lack of knowledge about yeast was a secondary matter but the world of brewing gradually became divided into two groups. On the one hand were the brewers who collected what they sensed was the ingredient responsible for the fermentation of the wort; having collected it they transferred it from one vat to another, thus always obtaining the same beer. On the other hand were the brewers who relied completely on nature, waiting for the wort to be "miraculously" transformed into beer, resulting in longer production times and no possibility of controlling it.

The second was the more fascinating approach, that of spontaneous fermentation that put up a fierce resistance, a little like the Gallic village of Asterix. In spite of all kinds of hardships and severe blows caused by legal vagueness and industrialization it survives today in a small area between Brussels and the Pajottenland (south-west of Brussels, along the river Senne). In the past there were many brewers in the Belgian capital and its surroundings who produced Lambic beer, that is, beer with spontaneous fermentation, but today only a handful are left. In Brussels itself just one has survived, Cantillon. It is still owned and managed by the same family: today the owner is Jean Van Roy, great-grandson of the founder Paul Cantillon, who continues to run the in-house Lambic production, assembling the Gueuze and making all the decisions for the company. The brewery has also become a museum of Lambic beer.

A visit to the Gueuze Museum (Rue Gheude 56, Anderlecht, Brussels), wandering through the maturation cellars, full of barrels, and seeing the copper brewing kettles and equipment dating from the 19th century, will explain this fascinating world better than a thousand words.

Spontaneous fermentation in beer is the quintessence of biodiversity; the wort ferments thanks to the yeasts and bacteria that are present naturally in the air: their concentration varies from brewery to brewery, from area to area. Today we are able to isolate yeasts and bacteria, to count them and to classify them into groups and subgroups but there are differences from year to year. All this is reflected in the beers, unique and closely linked to the cellars where they are created and developing with the flora that inhabits them.

Brewers do not have much room for maneuver. At the most they can work on the production of the wort, using

un-malted wheat for a large part of the cereal mixture, which with its starch helps the wild yeasts to take hold; and they can control the barrels, perhaps using them to provide a further element of character. But above all they must wait for nature to take its course. Apart from industrial systems that tend to denature the result, these beers are exclusively produced in the cold season, starting at the first frost and continuing until the beginning of spring. This is to prevent unwelcome bacteria from getting the upper hand over the favorite of the house, the *Brettanomyces* yeast, the protagonist of these beers. It goes into action with its many brothers (the various types of this "wild" yeast), lactic bacteria, acetobacteria and so on, each one with its own task to perform, making its own large or small but always fundamental contribution.

In the case of Cantillon alone, research scientists at the University of Louvain have identified over 100 different types of yeasts (several *Saccharomyces*, a very large number of *Brettanomyces*, and others), 27 different acetobacteria and 38 types of lactic bacteria that all contribute to the fermentation of the wort. This was a few years ago, but it already seems that the new actors of secondary importance have now appeared on the scene…

But spontaneous fermentation is not a characteristic of Pajottenland alone. In Flanders, so not far away, are the Reds of Flanders, a blend of a top-fermented beer and a fermentation with lactic and acetic bacteria in large oak vats in which the acetic touch, softened by the sweetness, dominates the aromatic sensations. Still in Flanders, Oud Bruin (Old Brown) beers are ones in which lactic bacteria have been added to the top-fermenting yeasts to give depth and broaden the gustatory spectrum.

Belgium is the repository of these traditions but that they have survived is also thanks to foreign markets, with the United States, the Scandinavia countries and Italy taking the lion's share. And not only as consumers. An ever-growing number of brewers in those countries are turning increasingly to long maturation in barrels, new or used, looking for aromatic profiles that recall those of spontaneous fermentations. This is to say that very few brewers are trying to achieve fermentation that is truly spontaneous… or nearly so!

## TOP FERMENTATION

"Top fermentation" describes the production of beers that are fermented by yeast working in the highest part of the fermentation vat, and usually at higher temperatures than are used for bottom fermentation, about 70 °F (20-22 °C). However, as we shall see there are exceptions.

They are commonly called Ales, the term for this type of fermentation, just as Lagers are bottom-fermented. It is a term that means everything and yet it means nothing: it simply identifies the type of yeast used, that generates an enormous family of beers that are very different from each other.

Top fermentation is typical of Great Britain and Belgium, and it has marked the great rebirth of beer in the United States and then in the rest of the world. It has created a kind of boundary between "supermarket" beers, the vast majority of which use bottom-fermenting yeast and are considered "flat" in terms of flavors and interest, and craft beers (artisanal or high quality beers) produced by independent micro-breweries, which often deliver a real explosion of flavors and character. In any case, not all bottom-fermented beers have the same flavor, and some of them are real masterpieces. Nor can it be said that a top-fermented beer is bound to be excellent… But of course this does not mean that a small producer cannot make great beers using either top fermentation or bottom fermentation!

Before yeasts were isolated and the chosen kind could be bought in practical packaging, beers were simply fermented by a mix of natural yeasts that for centuries had as it were selected themselves, adapting to particular working conditions (temperature and alcohol) with the fittest yeasts surviving. They "lived" in the same beers, where they proliferated, and they were reused from one batch to another in an endless chain, a bit like what used to happen (and is beginning to happen again) in the bakery with the "mother dough." These yeasts handed down from generation to generation are part of the strain now known as *Saccharomyces cerevisiae*, from which of course other more modern dough are descended, and these are called top-fermenting yeasts.

Britain was the first to turn brewing into an industrial process, replacing the look of the alchemical laboratory or farm that had been the standard previously. More recently Real Ales have prospered again and thanks to a great work of volunteers from the 1970s, they are still flourishing. Bitter, Porter, Stout and India Pale Ale were all born in Britain and then spread to Ireland, to Russia (Imperial Russian Stout), as well as having a new life in the United States. Top fermentation has proved to be a perfect match for English barley (and therefore malts) and English hops. Over time, the earthy hints of the hops and the biscuity-flavored malts were blended by the yeasts, which remained quite hidden in the taste, apart from occasional "burps" of sulfur and diacetyl (buttery notes) as the beer matures. These yeasts have also proved suitable for cask conditioning, the process that enables Anglo-Saxon breweries to make beer more quickly, since there is a relatively short time between the beer being brewed and ready to serve. It has also created professional publicans, who continue the work of the brewers by looking after the beer directly in their own cellars.

Belgium is the country where top-fermenting yeasts have shown their full potential, not only as a fermenting agent, but as the characteristic element of flavor. While in British beers the role of yeast is usually in the background as the creator of alcoholic content, in Belgium it is very often the prime contributor to the beer's taste.

To some extent it is a trait of the Belgian brewing world: when you cannot rely on nature to decide the character of the beers (spontaneous fermentation), yeasts are selected to do so directly.

Britain has been prominent for its research into the cultivation of barley and into malting techniques as well as studying hops. By contrast, Belgium has left these aspects almost in the background, focusing more on the study of yeast, almost at the cost of seeing hop plantations disappear (they have only recently been recovering). Over the years Belgian brewers have selected their own unique yeast, which can give a beer a signature that is unique to the brewery where it was made. Producers without a laboratory and who do not have their own yeast have great difficulty in recreating the same notes when they change to a new batch of *Saccharomyces* from a general supplier. Some breweries have a unique yeast that can work at different temperatures, thus making beers with flavor profiles that differ to a greater or lesser extent.

Some Belgian beers are, literally, yeast masterpieces: not only do they have very high levels of alcohol and attenuation that result in a pleasing dryness, but they also have esters that contribute strongly to the aroma and a good part to the flavor. Suffice it to say that the spicy, almost smoked notes of some Saison beers, the fruity notes of Dubbel, Quadrupel and other such styles, and the phenols of Tripel, are sensations that the right yeasts provide.

The Orval Trappist brewery has a micro-biology laboratory that monitors the yeast isolated years ago. Furthermore it is available to any brewer on request (as long as they go collect it directly). It is a unique yeast that is used for the only beer brewed in the monastery, quite unmistakable.

Even in Germany top-fermenting yeasts are used, particularly for wheat beers. In a Weizen (or Weissbier) that does so, the taste is punctuated by yeast: the sensations of ripe banana are the result of a chemical compound (isoamyl acetate) given off by the yeast as it works, as well as phenols that we perceive as cloves. Hops are there but not prominent, while the grist gives a mouthfeel with the astringency of wheat.

# BOTTOM FERMENTATION

Bottom-fermented beers are so called because they are made with yeasts that work at the bottom of the fermentation tanks, but they are commonly referred to as Lager, which is the German word for storage or a warehouse.

The term Lager does not identify styles or flavors (any more than the definition of Ale for top-fermenting beers does), and it is also widely used for beers that are produced industrially. But in fact this word takes us back to the dawn of their history, to the times when beers were matured for several weeks in the cellars and tunnels dug under the breweries, away from the heat. Since gas refrigeration systems had not yet been invented, the only way to keep beer cool was to put the barrels in these cellars, where the temperatures varied very little. Often further tunnels were dug which, towards the end of winter, were packed with ice taken directly from lakes or rivers nearby. This allowed the beers to be maintained at a temperature close to 32 °F (0 °C), the temperature needed to mature them best.

Those responsible for the creation of bottom-fermented beers as we know them today were the German Gabriel Sedlmayr and the Dane Emil Christian Hansen.

Sedlmayr's achievement was to import into Germany the mechanized method of beer production used in Britain in the 1830s, during the industrial revolution. He adapted it for Germany, bringing about the large-scale development of the historic Spaten brewery in Munich in Bavaria, and his methods then spread to the whole of the German brewing industry. For accuracy and consistency, Sedlmayr introduced the use of certain British production techniques, including using the saccharometer, to make the most of the ingredients and equipment. He also made changes in the malting process.

Hansen was a mycologist who was employed by Carlsberg in Copenhagen from 1870 until he died in 1909. Through his research he was the first to isolate a pure cell of the yeast that was responsible for the fermentation of the wort. This yeast was named *Saccharomyces carlsbergensis* after the brewery where it had been isolated. Through his studies, Hansen also discovered that it was possible to reproduce this yeast in the laboratory.

These two experiences, put together, give us the world of modern lagers, most of which are proudly displayed in colored bottles with gaudy labels on the shelves of supermarkets throughout the world.

But bottom fermentation is not only used for beers made by a rapid industrial process, where the marketing costs more than the ingredients. It is also used for craft beers. In general these are complex beers that require long ageing at very low temperatures, sometimes for two or three months, to reach their perfect balance with a clean, fragrant aroma. The yeasts used, due to the low temperatures at which they work—with inoculation at below 60 °F (15 °C) and maturation at about 32 °F (0 °C)—contribute little to the level of flavor or aroma. But they leave the field open (or rather they prepare it perfectly) for the flavor of hops from Hallertau, Tettnang and the other parts of Germany and Bohemia where these ingredients are grown, rather than for the malts. The long cellar (or refrigerated) ageing allows the yeast slowly to absorb any off-flavors as they are emitted. These can include diacetyl, which gives the beer an unpleasant sensation of fruity butter, and various sulfurous compounds that lead to effects ranging from the classic smell of rotten eggs to cooked vegetable notes. Having absorbed these off-flavors the yeast settles to the bottom, making the beer clear and a pleasure to the eye.

Some of the best session beers (beers that are easy to drink, usually a little bitter and low in alcohol) are part of this family, which includes

Pils, Hell and many others. In Franconia every brewery produces bottom-fermented beers that are then consumed in quantity in the adjacent tavern. Each brewery interprets the traditional beers (a long list including Ungespundet, Keller, Zwickl, Landbier, Pils, Lager, Export lager and many more, not forgetting Bock, Doppelbock and Schwartz) in its own way; starting from a common idea, the beers are incredibly different from each other. The German Beer Purity Law that over the centuries has controlled beer production has not led to bland uniformity, since it still leaves sufficient freedom for the brewers. But it does not control the quality of the beers, so they can still be very good or very bad, even though complying with the Purity Law.

Despite the advanced techniques introduced by Sedlmayr and the Purity Law, the world of bottom fermentation is still closely tied to the city from which the individual beers originate. This is mainly due to the characteristics of the water, resulting in different types of barley malts. These have created individual styles still known as Münchner, Dortmunder, Pils, from the city of Pilsen in Bohemia, and Vienna Lagers to the south.

The level of hygiene in a brewery that uses bottom-fermenting yeast must be worthy of an operating theater. This applies whether or not the fermentation tank is open to the air, without a cover. Most brewers have happily forgotten that in the not so distant past beers were matured in wooden barrels, inheriting aromas… and much else besides. Today brewers in their immaculate white coats walk on polished floors and are reflected in the shining steel of their equipment.

The whole world has been invaded by industrial lager, but high profile bottom-fermented production has flourished in response. In the United States, for instance, two new beer styles have been launched, American Pilsner Lager and Amber Lager, characterized by generous handfuls of American hops, reaching limits of bitterness and aromas beyond the original German lagers.

Italy has not held back and owes its renaissance in the field of brewing to some wonderful examples of bottom-fermented beers that, while maintaining strong roots in the traditional style, have managed to innovate with the characteristic flair of "Made in Italy." At one time the north east of Italy, under the rule of the Austro-Hungarian Empire, was dotted with breweries that were heavily influenced by the Austrian brewing tradition, not unlike the German one. This explains why bottom fermentation is still so common in the region. In general bottom-fermented craft beers are in the minority in Italy, but they are in most cases very interesting and well made. As a result the Italian national competition "Beer of the Year," organized by Unionbirrai, now includes an Italian Lager category for Italian beers that are clear and low in alcohol, inspired (but in a non-prescriptive sense) by the German brewing world.

The Netherlands in the course of its history has looked a little to the south and a little to the west. Some of the breweries in the German style and recently some Dutch brewers have begun to change their habits by renewing the ancient, deep-rooted traditions that lie behind the production of beer in their country. Apart from these examples, other regions of the country have mostly accepted the industrial versions, without adding much by way of experimentation or research.

# SERVING BEER

For good reason we believe that it is impossible to simplify and generalize, but if you want a simple rule that is always right for serving beer, our advice is… do as you like! You will never die from a badly served beer or one drunk ice-cold from the bottle!

If on the other hand, you want to enjoy it to the full, just relax: there is no single correct way to serve beer and only a small number of set reference points.

- The first, unarguably, is that serving beer is a delicate and important operation to optimize it for drinking (or if done wrong, spoiling it).
- The second is that all the factors involved are equally important and well-known: the temperature, the type of glass and its preparation, dispensing techniques (or pouring from the bottle) and the type of beer to serve.

We begin by identifying two major ways of serving beer: dispensing from kegs and pouring from bottles.

It is up to the expert publican to decide whether to serve the beer using a pressure pump, a hand pump or by gravity (in other words, served directly from the cask).

## DRAUGHT BEER

Draught dispensing is definitely the most widespread method of delivering beer and is based on the use of gas that is forcibly injected to create pressure within the hermetically sealed keg, pushing the beer through the cooled pipe that finally leads to the nozzle of the faucet. Obviously certified food-grade gas is used, such as carbon dioxide or carbon-nitrogen (a mixture of carbon dioxide and nitrogen). With this system, suitable for most styles of beer throughout the world, it is possible for the beer to be served quickly but badly, icy and over-carbonated. But by working more calmly and professionally, playing with the distance and tilt of the glass, it is possible to serve excellent beers with the correct carbon dioxide content and a beautiful head of foam, at the right temperature.

## THE HAND PUMP

The hand pump is a very traditional method of serving beer with its imposing lever and typical long nozzle, shaped like a swan's neck. It makes it possible to serve the beer even if the keg is further away, usually in the cool of the cellar or in a refrigerator underneath the bar. It works on a very simple principle: by manually pulling the lever, a vacuum is created that enables the beer to be sucked out of the cask. Sometimes a device called a "sparkler" is attached at the end of the nozzle. This has many small holes through which the beer passes under greater pressure with more turbulence, creating a large quantity of micro-bubbles that produce a very fine, compact, creamy foam. These will be relatively flat beers that do not make your stomach bloat and that are best appreciated not too cold. This type of dispensing can be used with many types of top-fermenting beers in the British and American style and it is quick to serve.

## FROM THE CASK BY GRAVITY

This is the most ancient and simplest way of serving beer and only needs a simple tap inserted into the barrel, through which the beer flows naturally as a result of the force of gravity. Evidently in this case as the beer pours out of the barrel, it is replaced by air and this in turn produces oxidation, which is why it is important to empty the barrel as soon as possible, especially if it is not refrigerated. Today this traditional technique is used mainly in Great Britain for serving Real Ale but you may also encounter this method elsewhere, such as in the German town of Bamberg, home to Rauchbier, or in Prague, the capital of the Pils. If you happen to witness the "ceremony" involved in opening a cask, perhaps wrapped in strange refrigerated jackets, do not be alarmed if someone approaches with a hammer or a mallet: it is only to insert the tap! There is no reason to worry unless his hand shakes so that he does not fit the tap properly; in that case there is the risk of splashing the people nearby with the precious liquid that is then lost. In general, do not expect beers served in this way to have a strong head of foam or to be very fizzy.

These three serving techniques must not been seen either as "right" or "wrong." The amount of foam, the temperature and the serving time are not absolutes.

Would you wear heavy mountain boots for an athletics competition? Or would you use a Ferrari for a cross-country outing? Let us say that everyone is entitled to do what they like, but the important thing is not to complain if your feet are sore and your car is dented! If served with a hand pump, you cannot expect a sparkling, ice cold beer. If served with a pressure pump with the glass tilted and close to the nozzle you can expect a beautiful, big head of foam, but possibly too an unpleasant bloated feeling. Once again it is necessary to know the different styles and the various customs and traditions of the various countries. In Belgium the head of foam is particularly impressive and it is the custom to "cut it" level with the rim of the glass using a small utensil such as a spatula. In Germany you may find the foam creamy and overflowing over the edge of the glass… and in England you may not find any foam at all! This does not mean anyone is wrong: as we said before, each to their own style and customs.

It is extremely important to use the right glass for each type of beer. Today each style of beer has its specific kind of glass and this can cause a little confusion…
The glass must be perfectly clean but without any trace of detergent or rinse aid since that would kill even the liveliest foam. It is also very important to rinse the inside of the glass generously with the coldest water possible to avoid giving the beer a thermal shock.

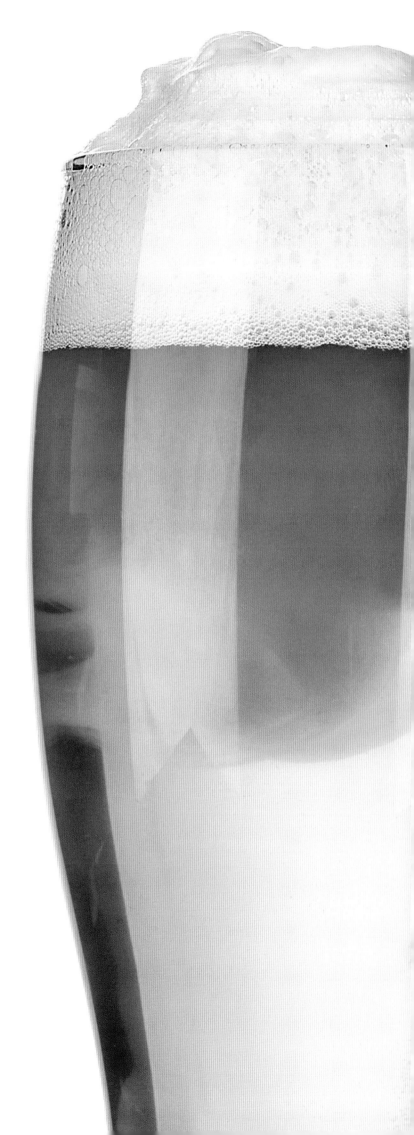

# BOTTLED BEER

When dealing with bottled beer, one of the most important conditions—even before talking about serving the beer—is the correct of storing it, especially if they are not pasteurized or re-fermented in the bottle. There is a rule that is generally accepted: the bottles must be stored vertically (unless they are sealed with a cork), in the dark (to prevent changes caused by direct light) and in a cool place. The length of time bottled beer can be kept varies according to the type. There are beers tht benefit from being drunk young such as APA or Hell and others like strong Barley Wine that mature for many years, continuing to develop and improve wonderfully.

When serving beer from the bottle the same care must be taken in selecting the glass. Choose the right kind of glass for the style of beer, wash it well and dry it thoroughly. While today one automatically thinks of glasses (that is, drinking vessels made of glass), in the past this was a luxury reserved for a select few. Most people drank their beer from jugs made of wood, clay or metal, or even from leather vessels coated with tar. The typical lidded tankards, that may seem rather folksy today, were actually very functional in the more rural context of the past or for drinking beer in the open, because the lid prevented insects and midges getting into the tankard. Those who claim that it was to prevent oxidation are not wrong but… ubi maior minor cessat ("where there is a major issue, the minor one becomes negligible")!

Another aspect to take into account when serving beer is that it should be at the right temperature. This can vary from 40 °F (5 °C) up to 65 °F (18 °C), or much higher in the case of Gluhbier, a spicy winter beer that is served hot like mulled wine.
Today beer labels and brewery websitesincreasingly often indicate the temperature at which the beer should be drunk; this is obviously an excellent point of departure, but generally it can be said that the simpler beers (such as the light Lagers) can be drunk rather cold while the more complex beers (for example the Belgian Dubbel and the English Old Ales) should be served at a temperature above 50-53 °F (10-12 °C). This is based on the principle that too low a temperature affects the taste.
The beer must be able exude its fragrances and the cold would prevent it from doing so. Too cold a temperature also influences the taste, because it prevents the correct perception of the flavors by the taste buds, which become as if paralyzed.
It must also be taken into account that the "serving temperature" should be that of the beer in the glass and therefore, to achieve it, it is necessary to take into account the ambient temperature, especially on hot summer days, as well the time needed to serve it.

At this point we have bottles of beer that have been perfectly brewed by the brewer, perfectly stored and prepared at the right temperature; and we have one or more suitable well-washed glasses.

Now we can open the bottle. Even this routine operation can be a treat, and one that provides further information. Let us get into the habit of listening to the more or less loud hissing of the pressure escaping; let us learn to watch the dense gas forming in the neck of the bottle and slowly, timidly escaping; let us observe all the bubbles rising to the surface, whether large or small and, if necessary, let us tilt the bottle slightly to increase the space available to them.

Finally let us pour the beer. Place the mouth of the bottle close to the glass, always leaving an inch or two between them. Then tilt the glass to an angle of about 45° and start pouring in such a way that beer slides along the side of the glass: not too roughly and not too slowly. As soon as the bottom of the glass is covered with beer and foam, straighten the glass and start pouring uninterruptedly and without hesitation into the middle of the glass until the glass is full. Do not worry about making a lot of foam (even 75% of the total volume of the glass) and, if necessary, adjust the distance between the glass and the bottle on the basis of the foam produced. But if there is too little foam, avoid the excesses of people who raise the bottle a couple of feet to show off their skilful aim: this is useless violence and it only means that the beer in question is naturally not highly carbonated: that is not a terrible thing! But also avoid pouring the beer with the glass tilted so far that it is almost horizontal, and do not pour the beer so slowly that it makes hardly any foam.

The production of foam releases carbon dioxide that would otherwise all remain in beer and therefore pass directly into the stomach, causing an unpleasant swelling sensation. So a nice layer of foam is not just aesthetically pleasing!

Try and test this on yourself and you will soon realize that a beer served in the right way is much easier and pleasanter to drink.

Also from the "tasting" point of view it is useful to lower the level of carbon dioxide in the glass slightly. On the rough taste buds, any excess of gas will quickly be released from the liquid in which it is contained, producing a multitude of little "explosions" which—in the same way as happens when the beer is too cold—will anaesthetize the taste buds and reduce their efficiency. We must give the foam sufficient time to recede and compact itself; then, holding the glass vertically, we continue pouring. Wait again and, if necessary, repeat these operations until there is the right level of beer and foam in the glass. Naturally this varies from style to style. But the photographs accompanying each style of beer presented in the next chapters will help you here.

Personally I do not worry too much about people who do not like foam: I always hope to convince them of the beauty of foam and I have fun showing them how easy it is to drink beer with a large head of foam. In order not to swallow the foam you just lift and tilt the glass and let the beer slide into your half-open mouth while the foam stops politely, resting on the upper lip or the moustache… in the case of those who have one.

# THE MAJOR COUNTRIES AND THE MAJOR STYLES OF BEER

In this section we present many different styles of beer, separated into the countries and regions where they originated at the beginning of their history. It is important to remember that, while there are examples of beers produced by individual producers that are absolute masterpieces, they will never be a definitive example of a style, since every style contains a multitude of varied facets.

The names, labels and brands of beers, so striking and appealing, are the externals, the appearance, the outside "skin." They are obviously necessary for recognition purposes, but they can be restrictive when, as in this case, the object is rather to intrigue, not to provide answers but to raise questions and to stimulate the eternal quest to taste and discover the best beer of the world—which may be a different one for every individual. This is why we decided to give priority to the styles of beer and what lies beneath the skin, to bring you the heart, the soul and the DNA of the various types of beer.

Styles incorporate a set of characteristics and objective parameters such as color, alcohol content, acidity-sweetness-bitterness, flavor, and aroma, that are then more or less freely interpreted by individual brewers. Although constantly evolving, describing styles of beer does honor to the past and their descriptions create a common ground between the producer and the consumer.

In any case, this survey of styles will be useful if you are someone whodoes not like buying or tasting beers "in the dark," or if you would like an opinion on a particular beer that you failed to enjoy, or if you are planning to take the path of the "beer hunters." For even more extensive guidance, if you are a big fan of rankings, by visiting websites such as www.ratebeer.com, www.beeradvocate.com, or www.untappd.com, you can read the opinions of others as well contributing your own, writing reviews of any beer you have tasted. On websites such as these you will find an enormous amount of material: thousands of breweries, hundreds of thousands of beers, millions of comments.

Obviously no tasting license is required for the you to make your own contribution… but do so with discretion!

In the following pages you will find details of numerous types of beer, from the most famous to ones that are little known, categorized according to the country or region in which they are produced. We have used the same categories in each entry, since this will enable you to make comparisons and to create your own personal classification. For each beer we shall give following information:

FAMILY: the type of fermentation used (top, bottom, or spontaneous).
CATEGORY: from which of the main international families it originated.
STYLE: the particular recipe and production method used (depending on the geographic area, tradition, etc.).
ORIGIN: the country or geographic area from which it originates.

For each type we shall also give a short history, including some unusual or interesting anecdotes, and how it came to be what it is today.

PRODUCTION

For each beer, we shall tell you the techniques, ingredients (and secrets…) used to produce it in this way. For this particular section, we advise you to refer to the glossary for the many technical terms you will come across here.

CHARACTERISTICS

These are the typical elements that distinguish a style. They may be present in the beer to a greater or lesser extent, depending on the individual brewer's interpretation of the style. In this part, because of the large number and diversity of the characteristics of each beer, it is a little difficult to stick to standard pattern. Therefore let us say that in a discursive manner we shall attempt to examine a series of aspects that we shall try to list in a set order, aware that for certain beers we shall give precedence to aromas, for others to the sensations on the palate, while for yet others we shall dwell more on the suggested accompaniments… Here are the typical characteristics of a beer:

**Appearance**: how the foam and the liquid part look (color, consistency etc.)
**Aroma**: the various fragrances that are perceived in the nose.
**Flavor**: what flavors are perceived when drinking a beer and what kind of body.
**Mouthfeel**: the sensation and taste that remain in the mouth after drinking the beer.
**Alcohol content**: the amount of alcohol contained in the beer expressed as a percentage by volume.
**Pairing**: something traditional, something special or something strange… just a suggestion, it is up to you to experiment!

# BELGIUM

Belgium, one of the countries with the greatest and longest-running brewing traditions, has always been associated with beer and it is dotted with breweries and beer gardens. It is the native land of Gambrinus, the legendary figure adopted as the "patron saint" of beer. Various traditions over the years hold that he was king of Flanders, a cup-bearer in the court of Charlemagne, the inventor of beer with hops and much else.

At the start of the 20th century there were over 3,300 breweries but by the end of the same century the number had drastically diminished with little more than 100 breweries still operating. After the crisis in the sector and also to some extent an identity crisis, there was a turning point at the start of the new millennium when a few young brewers began introducing new products, so giving a new impulse to brewing. Today the number of brewers is growing again and though the splendid days of the past are still a distant memory, the small producers, as well as exporting their beers, have re-conquered parts of the market, replacing a proportion of the industrial lagers that had invaded the Belgian market. This went back some time: after the Second World War Belgium responded to the invasion of beers with low alcohol content and bland taste that were spreading all over the world by producing a number of beers with a high alcohol content that masked the bitter notes but preserved the spicy notes produced by the yeasts.

Today young and dynamic brewers such as De Ranke (Flanders), De la Senne (Brussels, the capital) and La Rulles (Wallonia), to mention just one from each region, are rewriting present-day Belgian brewing history. They are making beers based on modern concepts, inspired by beers with a very old tradition that have now disappeared, in which the bitterness of hops once again plays a major role as well as the yeasts. This in turn

has encouraged the cultivation of hops, with plantations punctuating the countryside with the traditional poles along which the hops climb during the summer months. The universities too have contributed to this new impetus, making their microbiology laboratories available to brewers who have not got one, helping them to isolate the yeast itself, and ensuring that their beers have a unique profile and signature.

Belgian brewing is also famous for its Lambic beers (see the chapter on Spontaneous fermentation), a heritage of ancestral beers that nearly fell into oblivion because of the dwindling number of producers and blenders (enterprises that bought Lambic beer and left it to mature it in their own cellars, then blending it with several vintages to create their own Gueuze). Today this sector is extremely healthy, particularly because of the great demand from abroad, while the home market is having a little trouble and many of the typical little cafés of Pajottenland have had to close their doors. Today the temples of these beers are the two bars Moeder Lambic, one in the center of Brussels and the other in the historic district of St Gilles, that offer a truly impressive selection of Lambic, Kriek, Gueuze (and other remarkable beers, all Belgian of course), and de Grote Dorst in Eizeringen, a pub that only opens on Sunday morning with a really incredible cellar of Gueuze and Lambic, including many old vintages.

Trappist beers are also typical of the Belgian beer panorama: at least six monasteries of the Cistercian Order produce beer in the Belgium. This can cause confusion: you will often hear people speaking of Trappist beers as a style of beer, when in fact the hexagonal label "Authentic Trappist Product" indicates that the beers were produced within the walls of the monastery and that the production was under the control of the monks (not necessarily meaning that the master brewer was a monk). The profits are devoted to good works, not to enriching the monastery itself.

# SAISON

FAMILY: TOP FERMENTATION
CATEGORY: BELGIAN ALE
STYLE: SAISON
ORIGIN: BELGIUM, WALLONIA

Saison beers are historic beers created in the farms of Wallonia, the French-speaking part of Belgium. Named after the French word for "season," they were originally rather ordinary beers: the objective was to quench the thirst of agricultural day laborers during the summer months and to pay them in part. So what was required was a beer that could be kept during the hottest months while remaining pleasant and refreshing. The alcohol content in those days was very low and each farm producing this beer had its own recipe that probably changed from year to year depending on the ingredients available. More to the west, in northern France, they supplanted the Bières de Garde that had a much higher alcohol content.

## PRODUCTION

Top-fermenting yeasts, suitable for working at high temperatures, are characteristics and help the wort to become a 5 to 7% abv beer. In many cases the spicy notes are obtained by adding an infusion of spices (such as pepper, cumin, Guinea pepper, coriander and others). Continental hops play a fundamental part so far as both bitterness and aroma are concerned. The cereal grist can also contain wheat and un-malted spelt.

## CHARACTERISTICS

Usually pale orange, the color can range from straw yellow to amber with coppery reflections. In many cases the beer has not been filtered so it may not be completely transparent. The foam is usually plentiful, compact and persistent.

The phenolic and spicy aromas of the yeast and other spices merge into a delicate herbaceous, floral bouquet of hops with long-lasting light malted notes and a clean lemony fruitiness.

On the palate the body is medium-light with a high carbonation that gives the beer a definite liveliness. It is accompanied by a moderately bitter finish and a long aftertaste, sometimes piquant, with peppery, herbaceous and lemony notes.

This is a beer that varies enormously depending on the producer but with a characteristic, refreshing light sharpness.

Alcohol content: 5-7% abv.
Pairing: seafood salad and crudités.

# BIÈRE BLANCHE

FAMILY: TOP FERMENTATION - WHEAT BEER
CATEGORY: BELGIAN ALE
STYLE: BIÈRE BLANCHE
ORIGIN: BELGIUM

A historic beer, it dates back to the Middle Ages before there were hops to flavor the beers and "gruyt" was used instead.

Having almost fallen into oblivion by the middle of the 20th century, it was revived by Pierre Celis. When he saw the last producer of wheat beer closing down in his town of Hoegaarden in Flanders, he decided to leave his job in order to revive this ancient specialty.

Today it is a very widespread type and particularly appreciated for its reviving freshness.

## PRODUCTION

Typically produced with a large quantity of un-malted soft winter wheat (up to 50% of the cereals used), its flavors come from coriander and bitter orange zest (Curaçao) and a top-fermenting yeast with very distinctive aromatic characteristics.

## CHARACTERISTICS

Very pale yellow, veering towards white because of its strong opalescence created by the presence of yeast in suspension and the use of wheat, with an abundant, dense and rather persistent white foam.

It has a delicate aroma of honey with aromas of citrus fruit and spices that must never be too invasive.

The body is a medium-light but well-rounded; it is expected to display a certain intensity of taste but also a dry, clean finish.

A light beer, very refreshing and thirst-quenching, it is a splendid drink for a summer evening.

Alcohol content: about 5% abv.
Pairing: poultry, fish and shellfish.

# BELGIAN GOLDEN STRONG ALE

FAMILY: TOP FERMENTATION
CATEGORY: BELGIAN STRONG ALE
STYLE: BELGIAN GOLDEN STRONG ALE
ORIGIN: BELGIUM

These beers are the "lay version" of the Trappist Tripel, created in the Moortgat brewery after the Second World War to counteract the commercial success of the industrially produced lagers, the very attractive golden colors of which they wanted rather shamelessly to reproduce. Very soon the beers were given "devilish" and "infernal" names and labels, partly in honor of their founder (in Flemish dialect "Duvel" means "devil") and partly for their deceptiveness: they look like innocent blondes, they go down extremely easily but then… they hit you with their high alcohol content that, as if by magic, you only become aware of when you have finished it.

## PRODUCTION
They are based on Belgian yeasts tolerant of alcohol that bring to the fore their fruity esters, spiciness and fusel alcohols; on the Pale Pilsner type malts for their color; on the addition of sugars to increase the alcohol content but without making it heavy-bodied; and on noble hops for the aroma.

## CHARACTERISTICS
The color is a beautiful golden yellow with very abundant foam: it is a very white, persistent foam that tends to stick to the glass.
The high carbonation helps to bring the varied aromas of this type out of the glass: fruit (apples, pears and oranges), spices (pepper) and the floral notes of hops.
In the mouth the scented, fruity, spicy notes combine delightfully with a light maltiness and a marked bitterness. This bitterness, together with the high level of effervescence and the relatively light body, produces a pronounced dry finish.
A great style of beer that is both complex and delicate. Truly diabolical!

Alcohol content: about 7.5-10 % abv.
Pairing: grilled red meat.

# FLEMISH RED ALE

FAMILY: TOP FERMENTATION (MATURED IN WOOD)
CATEGORY: SOUR ALE
STYLE: FLEMISH RED ALE
ORIGIN: BELGIUM

These are very old traditional beers from West Flanders. They have a wonderful color and an interesting acidity, more acetic than the Lambic beers and very reminiscent of a wine.

## PRODUCTION

After the typical fermentation, the beer is left to mature for two years in large oak barrels where it develops its acidulous character thanks to the natural presence of colonies of Brettanomyces, Acetobacteria and lactobacillus that continue to transform it slowly (in a different way from Lambic beers, because here there is no "spontaneous fermentation"). The beers aged in this way are then blended with young beers, to balance their acidity and make them more mellow and complex.

## CHARACTERISTICS

They have an intense Bordeaux color, tending towards chestnut, that is reminiscent of the great wines of Burgundy, with a medium and persistent white to ivory foam. The aroma is unmistakable and in perfect harmony with the flavor: fruity and very complex with notes of black cherries, redcurrants and plums. There are light notes of malt reminiscent of chocolate and a hint of vanilla, and an acidity that would be almost pungent if it had not been mitigated by a certain sweetness from the caramel flavor of the malt.

This is an intriguing and unique beer that should be approached slightly intellectually before enjoying it: the sight and perfume alone will provide pleasure even to those who cannot appreciate its sharp taste.

Alcohol content: about 4.6-6.5 % abv.
Pairing: as an aperitif but also with a cherry tart.

# OUD BRUIN OR FLANDERS BROWN

FAMILY: TOP FERMENTATION (MIXED)
CATEGORY: SOUR ALE
STYLE: OUD BRUIN
ORIGIN: BELGIUM

Closely related to the Flemish Red Ale but typical of the beers of east Flanders, the "Old Browns" have a darker color, typical of the days when toasting the malts was a process that was hard to control. Boiling the wort for a very long time over a direct flame tended to caramelize the sugars, leading to a less pronounced acidity than its western cousins because it was balanced by the sweetness of the malts: practically a sweet-and-sour beer.

PRODUCTION
This beer is also left to mature for a long time, not in wooden barrels but in stainless steel vats and at room temperature. It is acidified by the addition of lactic bacteria or acidulated malts and of water rich in carbonates and magnesium, adding further emphasis to this particular profile.

CHARACTERISTICS
Chestnut-colored with reddish reflections, it has an intense, complex aroma of malt (caramel, toffee, chocolate), and of ripe and dried fruit (black cherries, prunes, figs, dates and raisins) with subtle acetic touches (less than the Flemish Red Ale style).
It is more straightforward and hedonistic than the other acid beers but it should always be approached with an open mind and an interest in new horizons.

Alcohol content: about 5-8% abv.
Pairing: game and venison.

# DUBBEL AND TRIPEL

FAMILY: TOP FERMENTATION
CATEGORY: BELGIAN STRONG ALE
STYLE: DUBBEL AND TRIPEL
ORIGIN: BELGIUM

Dubbel and Tripel, often associated with mysterious double and triple fermentation, rather than double and triple malt, are actually produced in the Trappist abbey of Westmalle. Three beers are produced there, one not very alcoholic beer, made for consumption in the monastery, another a little more alcoholic with toasted malts, and the third one decidedly more alcoholic. The barrels in which they were matured were marked with a single, double or triple X, hence the names Extra, Dubbel (which goes back to the Middle Ages and was revived in the abbey of Westmalle in the second half of the 19th century) and Tripel (introduced in about 1950).

## PRODUCTION

The ingredients are water, several types of barley malt (in the complex grist of the Dubbel beers, these are also toasted and caramelized, while the Tripel uses basic and aromatic malts), continental hops, frequently candy sugar or white sugar (to increase the alcohol without affecting the body), and most importantly, top-fermenting yeast. They are rigorously re-fermented in the bottle, in the Belgian tradition.

## CHARACTERISTICS

The Dubbel beers, between 6 and 7.5% abv, range in color from amber to intense coppery hues and they have a creamy, persistent head of foam. The warm fragrances with notes of fruit and toffee are the result of a combination of malts and yeasts. The medium body is in perfect balance with alcoholic warmth, making it a splendid drink.
The Tripel beers, between 7.5 and 9.5% abv, have an intense golden color, clear, with an abundant, persistent foam. It has a spicy, fruity nose (citrus, apricot or apricot jam and sometimes banana), with a light floral aroma of hops. They reflect the perfect harmony between the malts and the work of the yeast.
The dryness make them dangerously easy to drink in view of their high alcohol content.

Pairing: both Dubbel and Tripel are perfect with cheese. They also go well with a carbonade flamande or game stew.

# LAMBIC

FAMILY: SPONTANEOUS FERMENTATION
CATEGORY: LAMBIC
STYLE: LAMBIC
ORIGIN: BELGIUM - PAJOTTENLAND

Lambic beers were born in a small region stretching from Brussels along the river Senne (which today crosses the city mostly underground) through Pajottenland. In this region the concentration of wild yeasts, in particular those of the Brettanomyces family, is extremely high. This means that brewers can still today produce beers with spontaneous fermentation without the inoculation of wild yeasts, just leaving nature to take its course. Because of the nature of these beers, the more traditional brewers only produce beer during the cold season, more or less from October to the end of March, depending on the years.

PRODUCTION
Besides water, the ingredients of a Lambic beer include malted barley, 40% un-malted wheat and aged hops, that have thereby lost their bitter, aromatic profile but not their natural conservation properties. The cooling process lasts a whole night and it takes place in the open in a large tank, wide but not deep. Then the wort is transferred into barrels, generally used ones, where it will ferment and mature for a long period that ranges from one to four years.

CHARACTERISTICS
Pale yellow to golden in color and slightly opalescent, typically without foam, Lambic beers have aromas reminiscent of a cellar (such as salami skins, used playing cards, leather, horse saddles) and citrus fruit. Older versions also develop fruity (apple) and honey notes.
It is sharp in the mouth with lactic acid notes but its light body and sourness make it very drinkable. A Lambic is a complex beer that is not to everybody's taste, but it is fascinating and extremely pleasant once you are used to it. Not a beer but... a Lambic!

Alcoholic content: about 5-6% abv.
Pairing: a good salami.

There are also other versions of Lambic including some to which up to 30% fruit (cherries, raspberries, grapes, peaches or blackcurrants) has been added (image right). These versions are fermented in bottle and are a combination of various fruit Lambics, some younger and some older, blended together in the same way as Gueuze.
This category also includes Gueuze itself (image left), a beer that is also fermented in bottle and made by mixing a young Lambic with one or more other Lambics that have been aged for two or three years.

# ENGLAND

England is one of the countries with the most important and longest-established brewing tradition that is well documented by numerous historical and archeological findings. We probably owe one of the most universal terms referring to beer to this country: Ale. This term, which today generally refers to all beers produced by top-fermenting yeasts, is thought to be derived from the ancient English word "ealu," a drink made from cereals that was already mentioned in the 8th century in Beowulf, the most famous Anglo-Saxon epic poem.

There was an important change in beer production in the Middle Ages when Henry VIII decided to curtail the power of the Catholic Church by closing down monasteries and convents, thus also removing their right to make beer. Since then the tradition of the so-called abbey beers only survived on the continent, while in England only lay people (and very often these were women) were in charge of fermenting barley, including on a domestic level. England has always paid more attention to raw materials than to the production techniques, which are famously simple, fast and rational.

English brewers learnt to "modify" the water in order to obtain better beers. Once they had found that, using the same recipe, the London beers, still known today as Bitter, were very much better if produced in Burton-on-Trent, they tried to understand the reason. It turned out to be the particular composition of the water in Burton-on-Trent, which is particularly rich in gypsum. London brewers then started adding this saline element to the London water, which lacked this particular element, so as to make it as similar as possible to the water in Burton-on-Trent. The results were so positive that this process, now used throughout the world, became known as Burtonization.

This also explains why London brewers guard their recipes so jealously: many have been written in a code known only within the brewery, indicating the saline correction made to the water.

The English also carried out important research into the cultivation of barley with the introduction of new species, selected ad hoc for some of their beers. They also studied the malting processes, such as Maris Otter and Golden Promise, processes that were named after two specifically selected types of barley; they are not particular types of malt, as many believe, both being Pale malts.

Although hops only became established after 1500, the tradition of English hops is a distinguished one. Ancient varieties such as Fuggle and Golding have written the history of English beer and they are the foundation of various new hybridizations.

Today we know everything about hops and crossings between the various types are the order the day, but there was a time when it was not so. Wye College in Kent, a department of the agricultural faculty of London University, then part of Imperial College until it closed in 2009, was a pioneer in the study of these plants. Its work provided the foundation for the research that is at the basis of every new species from the United States to New Zealand.

Most of the English beers, all strictly top-fermenting beers, seemed to be specially made to be drunk by the gallon from the cask in public houses, the famous pubs patronized by reserved English people who, pint by pint, lose their phlegmatic air and begin to socialize. Still today in pubs local people continue to drink bitter, porter, mild and brown ale at cellar temperature in large quantities. The beers are served from the pump (that is, without the assistance of $CO_2$ to "thrust" it into the glass), and accompanied by traditional dishes or quick snacks. The pub is the best place to drink and enjoy company, although it may not always be the best place to eat.

The fact that traditional Anglo-Saxon beers still survive today is due above all to the work of an association of volunteers, CAMRA (CAMpaign for Real Ale). This organization fought, and continues to fight, to preserve English beers, the Real Ales, through tireless campaigning, pressing for pubs to become "free houses," that is, independent from breweries and therefore free to choose the beers they want to offer to their patrons.

# ENGLISH BARLEY WINE

FAMILY: TOP FERMENTATION
CATEGORY: STRONG ALE
STYLE: ENGLISH BARLEY WINE
ORIGIN: ENGLAND

English Barley Wines are the English Ales with the highest alcohol content and the most full-bodied. They are opulent, complex and challenging, rich in malt and hops, and they can be kept and matured for very many years, evolving so much over the years that it has become customary for producers to indicate on the bottle the year the beer was produced and also the recommended date of consumption, a fact that, in countries where this is obligatory by law, has a real symbolic value. Do not be surprised to see labels displaying the words "To be consumed before the end of the world!"

The term "Barley Wine" is relatively recent and dates back to the end of the 19th or beginning of the 20th century. At that time the term did not yet refer to a style but simply indicated that it was the strongest beer of the house. The first brewery to use it was Bass Brewery with its Strong Ale No. 1, but the tradition of strong beers is an ancient one and is derived from the old March beers, produced at the end of the production season.

CHARACTERISTICS

These ales contain many malts of different kinds, embittering English hops such as the Target and yeasts that are very tolerant of alcohol. After their long fermentation these beers need a long period of rest, sometimes in wooden barrels as was the case in the past. They vary enormously in color, ranging from pale amber to brown, but never as dark as black. They are usually a little carbonated and their foam is not a conspicuous feature. On the other hand, they have an intensely aromatic profile with ethyl notes, notes of honey, fruit (particularly dried fruit), caramel, toffee and molasses; the hop is very perceptible in the younger beers but its aroma decreases with the years when micro-oxidation creates vinous impressions similar to port and sherry. When tasting these beers one is struck by their full, almost chewable, body, the complex smoky sweetness of the malts, the notes of dried fruit, the bitterness and spiciness of the hops, accompanied by a long and sustained finish with an alcohol that does not burn but warms the chest.

Here we have the opposite of the Bitter beers: a glass of Barley Wine may be enough to accompany and satisfy you during a whole winter evening together with a good book in front of the fire.

Alcohol content: about 8-13% abv.

Pairing: a typical meditation beer, it can be sipped slowly without food, but it will also surprise you when accompanying blue cheeses or spicy ones.

# ENGLISH IPA

FAMILY: TOP FERMENTATION
CATEGORY: INDIA PALE ALE (IPA)
STYLE: ENGLISH IPA
ORIGIN: ENGLAND

This is a very hoppy, traditional style of beer that is today experiencing an exciting revival in several countries (although a little less in its own country) thanks to the innovations introduced by the more modern aromatic hops. Although not a beer for everyone, it is probably at the height of its reputation among beer enthusiasts and many brewers.

Originally, at the end of the 18th century, India Pale Ale (IPA) was the strong March beer that was transported to India (hence its name): this was because its alcoholic strength and generous hop content enabled it to survive the long sea journey. When in the next century many English brewers lost the important Russian market because of the introduction of higher taxes, they concentrated on the increasingly flourishing market of India, exporting beers similar to those they were already sending there but paler and lighter, as was the fashion at the time. The Pale Ales of Burton-on-Trent, well attenuated, slightly more alcoholic and much richer in hops, were the most successful and so became the standard for this style of IPA that soon also became very popular in England under the name of Pale Ale.

CHARACTERISTICS

Today IPAs are lighter than they were then, between golden and amber-colored, with a fine-grained foam, compact and persistent. They are beers based on hops and the dry-hopping technique is also used during the maturation period in order to control its aroma (floral, spicy, herbaceous, resinous) and the flavor. But there must be no coarseness in the bitterness of the finish, and the malty component and the body must be sufficiently evident to ensure a perfect balance of flavor. These are original beers, full of character, that can surprise and bewitch with their fresh, intense notes of hops.

Alcohol volume: about 5-7.5% abv.
Pairing: generally excellent with hot and spicy foods of all kinds.

# ORDINARY BITTER

FAMILY: TOP FERMENTATION
CATEGORY: ENGLISH PALE ALE
STYLE: ORDINARY BITTER (OR SIMPLY BITTER)
ORIGIN: ENGLAND (LONDON)

The Bitters are Ales that can be bitter, as the name suggests, but in fact in today's vast present-day panorama of styles they are not particularly bitter, having long ago been superseded in this respect by other more "aggressive" and definite styles such as that of India Pale Ale. But in the historical evolution of the English production, the term Bitter was introduced in the 19th century to emphasize that these Ales were very hoppy and therefore more bitter than the other more widespread beers: the Porters and Milds. The other important difference was the color: after centuries of beers that were brown as a result of being produced with brown malts prepared on wood fires, these were "paler," in fact amber-colored. They were also called Pale Ale because they were made with malts that had been dried more delicately using modern techniques. The terms Bitter Ale and Pale Ale were used indiscriminately to indicate the same thing: sometimes the bottled version was called Pale Ale while the same beer served from the cask was called Bitter Ale! Consequently there is much confusion between Bitters and Pale Ales… but it is nothing to worry about.

Historically there are several types of Bitter based on the alcohol level and structure: Best Bitter, Special Bitter, Extra Special Bitter, and Strong Bitter. But today what is most important is to realize that there are new interpretations, developed by small independent brewers who emphasize the characteristics of this style compared to the classic versions in "Real Ale" style.

## CHARACTERISTICS

Ordinary Bitters are the lightest and simplest of the family: they are all top-fermented beers, usually with a more or less intense golden/amber color and a pleasant, well-balanced aroma. They taste of malt (and of caramel) and of fresh hops (floral, resinous and spicy, typical of Kent), with the fruity notes of the yeast esters always evident. They are beers that are easy to drink thanks to their light body and gently bitter finish.

The real "session beer" of England, Bitter should be drunk young and served at cellar temperature, from the pump or tapped from the cask in a beautiful pub.

Alcohol content: about 3-3.5 abv.
Pairing: good friends, a good pub, roast chicken with potatoes—or another pint of Bitter.

# BROWN PORTER

FAMILY: TOP FERMENTATION
CATEGORY: PORTER
STYLE: BROWN PORTER
ORIGIN: ENGLAND

This dark ale is derived from the old Brown Ales of 18th-century London. The success of this product was so incredible that it became the subject of many myths and legends even when it was first launched. It is said that at the time the custom among the poorest workers was to go to the pub and ask for "three threads," that is, a pint of which one third was a cheap, light beer, another third was a stronger and more expensive "ale," and the last third was the prestigious and exclusive "twopenny," of which they could not afford a whole pint. But this custom was also a nightmare for the publican who lost time as a result, slowing down the service and irritating his patrons. To speed up the pulling of a pint of "three threads," a publican had the idea of mixing these three beers in advance. This blend subsequently became known as "Porter" because it was extremely popular among porters and laborers working in the ports and towns.

This is a delightful little story but the facts are quite different. First, Porter was the first industrially produced beer: cheap, produced on a large scale and sold "ready to drink," unlike all the other beers that finished their maturation process in the pub cellars. The other interesting point is that after nearly three centuries as a most successful beer, Porter was suddenly considered "down-market," losing much of its original popularity so much that in the end it was completely displaced by the stronger Stout.

Porter beers are more or less dark brown, with dark red reflections and a creamy-colored medium-persistent foam. The dominant note is that of roast malt, delicate and mellow, but not "burnt," and to a lesser degree there are also notes of caramel, coffee and chocolate. The hops are more obvious in the American versions than in the English ones, both as far as bitterness and aroma are concerned. The medium-light body and good attenuation make it a very approachable dark ale.

Brown Porter is the Cinderella of the Porter beers, lighter, easier and more delicate than Robust Porter and Baltic Porter (also known as Imperial Porter).

Alcohol content: about 4-5.4% abv.
Pairing: with braised beef and beef stew (previously marinated in Porter).

# MILD

FAMILY: TOP FERMENTATION
CATEGORY: ENGLISH BROWN ALE
STYLE: MILD
ORIGIN: ENGLAND

In the distant past the term Mild was used to designate beers that were sold "fresh," having just been made, without the long maturation undergone by the Old Ales that made them mellow and soft. After the First World War the term was used to define the lighter beers that in times of austerity were those most drunk because they were cheap. They filled the glasses of the English until after the Second World War but then declined in popularity in favor of the lighter and drier Pale Ales.

Today this style of beer no longer appeals and there is very little demand for it, except by beer enthusiasts. Some years ago the English association CAMRA launched a campaign, symbolically entitled "Save the Mild," that among other things proposed to make May the month of Mild ("Mild Month May"). For that month all the local branches of the association try to persuade publicans to include at least one Mild in their list of beers and to organize special tasting events promoting Milds. This clearly indicates the delicate state of health of this now very unfashionable style of beer at time when the market is dominated by hoppy beers.

CHARACTERISTICS

Milds range from dark brown, almost black, to amber-colored. Their character also varies: some are dark ales with a slightly wintery character, with roast and caramelized notes, others are lighter, refreshing and thirst-quenching, and a perfect pairing for any dish.

They all have a low alcohol content and a medium-light body, in which the malted, sweet notes dominate, although there can also be a light hint of hops both in the nose and on the palate. They may also have low levels of diacetyl.

They are beers that do not give their best in bottles, so they should be served from the pump.

Alcohol content: under 4.3% abv.

Pairing: white cream cheese, also sheep and goat's cheese, the slight acidity of which will counter-balanced by the sweetness and maltiness of the Milds.

# RUSSIAN IMPERIAL STOUT

FAMILY: TOP FERMENTATION
CATEGORY: STOUT
STYLE: RUSSIAN IMPERIAL STOUT
ORIGIN: ENGLAND

These Stouts are the most powerful and challenging in the category; the adjective "Russian" reflects the great popularity of these Ales at the Court of the Russian tsars in the 19th century, that for a long time was a serious export market, as were the countries on the Baltic sea.

All the ingredients in this beer are used in large quantities and they are all very important to ensure its complexity. They are very dark and tend to be an opaque black because of the very generous use of the entire range of dark roast malts. The bouquet has strong notes of hops, with a bitter finish when the rich bitter aroma of the hops combines with that of the dark malts.

## CHARACTERISTICS

These beers are very aromatic as a result of the yeast that produces strong fruity esters of cooked plums and sultanas as well as other dried fruits and nuts. They are very alcoholic, very full-bodied, very intense, and very complex. They could be described as darker sisters of Barley Wine, and like them they are very long in the mouth. They have everything, and in the case of the modern version produced in the United State, they have even more.

Tasting an Imperial Russian Stout requires a little awareness and training but if you like risks and you want to try them… don't hesitate! If you survive the dimensional tunnel in which you find yourself descending, you could find yourself in raptures.

Alcohol content: about 8-12% abv.
Pairing: chocolate pudding or coffee.

IRELAND

Ireland has a strong brewing tradition, equal to that of the Anglo-Saxon countries, but clearly it is impossible to think of Ireland without picturing a full pint of dark beer with a thick, dense foam, and a clover leaf drawn on top of it. With all due respect to the Irish, it has to be said that Stout was born in London, although thanks to Arthur Guinness and his breweries it is now famous all over the world. And today, when we talk of Dublin, as well as James Joyce, there also comes to mind the golden harp that appears on all Guinness merchandising. The company was founded in 1759 and since then it has introduced quite a few novelties into the world of brewing: first, dispensing beer with a carbon dioxide-nitrogen blend that "pushes" the beer into the glass without excessive gassing as well as creating the characteristic creamy foam. Cans and bottles have devices to achieve the same effect, as if you were sitting in the pub.

Unlike Britain, a country that is a ferment of new brews, re-interpretations of original styles, and new openings of both pubs and breweries, Ireland has remained much as it was, hidden behind its centuries-old tradition. It should be stressed that consumptions has not dropped in spite of the economic crisis that has hit the island, and it is very likely that when this has passed, breweries will become stronger and innovate again.

For now you can certainly enjoy the traditional pubs that are located in the big cities and in the little villages, immersed in the green countryside. There you can sip pints of Irish Red Ale, perhaps reading James Joyce's *Dubliners*, picturing the Dublin of old, or watching a rugby match broadcast on the screens, admiring the successes of the national team with the green jersey.

# IRISH RED ALE

FAMILY: TOP FERMENTATION
CATEGORY: IRISH AND SCOTCH ALE
STYLE: IRISH RED ALE
ORIGIN: IRELAND

While Stout was born in London, Irish Red represents the true essence of Irish brewing, and also a response to the extra special bitter of the island. It has a more sustained alcohol content than the beers of London and its surroundings, and a character that owes more to malt than to hops.

## PRODUCTION

Irish Reds are made with a good dose of malts, local or English, Caramel and sometimes Roasted as well. The yeast is not particularly distinctive, but its presence can be felt with buttery notes (diacetyl) that, in small doses, is very acceptable. Like the yeast, English hops are also used sparingly, and in any case do not remain much in evidence: for bitterness, Roasted malts are used in preference. There are also some bottom-fermented versions.

## CHARACTERISTICS

It is amber in color, clear, with coppery highlights and normally a white foam. The sense of smell plays on aromas of caramel and toffee and sometimes toasted notes. The scents of yeast and hops are not present or are hidden by the notes of malts. The body is medium and the carbonation is moderate. The flavors hold up well: the sweet caramel and bitter notes from the malts are often accompanied by a "roasted" sensation that is made more evident by the dryness on the finish. In drinking, these are accompanied by pleasant toasted butter notes (due to the yeast).
These are beers that are easy to drink, suitable for any time of the day, especially the versions with lower alcohol content.

Alcohol: about 4-6% abv.
Pairing: perfect with meat dishes in the Irish tradition.

# DRY STOUT

FAMILY: TOP FERMENTATION
CATEGORY: STOUT
STYLE: DRY STOUT
ORIGIN: ENGLAND/IRELAND

Created to quench the thirst of the patrons of London pubs, following in the wake of the successful Porters, these were the more alcoholic version of the latter and were initially called Stout Porter. Today they have a lower alcohol content and owe their fame mainly to the Irish breweries of Arthur Guinness, of Beamish and of Murphy. In fact the beers drunk in Dublin and its surroundings are actually the Dry Stouts that struggle to survive in the rest of the world and in London are almost completely forgotten.
They are very hard to find in bottle but they are widely available on draught, which is how they are best drunk.

## PRODUCTION
The un-malted but roasted barley is responsible for both the color and dryness that is typical of these beers; sometimes barley flakes (never malted) are also used to make them creamier. The rest of the grist consists of Pale malts. The English hops are a fundamental ingredient that gives the beer its bitterness. The water must be quite soft and the attenuation of the yeast is fundamental to emphasize the sensation of dryness.

## CHARACTERISTICS
These stouts are dark, impenetrable, sometimes opaque, with a fine, creamy, persistent foam, the color of cappuccino. The aromas are variations on the theme of barley, chocolate, cocoa beans and carob, sometimes with notes of fruity esters produced by the yeast. The body is between medium-light and medium-full while the moderate carbonation, sometimes with moderate acidity, balances the dryness and bitter finish with a long aftertaste of notes of melting chocolate and coffee.

Alcohol content: about 4-5% abv.
Pairing: in spite of the low level of alcohol it is delicious with fatty dishes,
also smoked, barbecued, smoked cheeses, pastries
and coffee-flavored desserts.

# SCOTLAND

Scotland is famous for its whiskies, in particular for the peaty, Islay styles, rather than for its brewing tradition. In that whisky is the distillation of a cereal fermentation (in practice a beer made with a yeast specially chosen by the distilleries), without beer these distillations would not exist; and indeed the Scots are not adverse to drinking a pint of beer.

The Scots have a reputation for thrift, and instead of giving names to the styles of beer, they have simply categorized them according to how much they cost: from 60, 70, 80 or 90 shillings, a term that has survived even after the disappearance of the shilling when the currency was decimalized. The 90 is also known as Scotch Ale or Wee Heavy, being the most alcoholic (up to 10%), but the most commonly drunk are the session beers, namely the 60 and 70 (with an alcohol content between 2.5% and 3.9%).

Probably again for economic reasons, their beers are characterized by malts (locally produced) rather than by hops that would have to be imported from England. The result are beers with a much stronger taste of malt and a fuller body, as well as being darker than their English cousins.

Scotland is experiencing a great brewing renaissance thanks to the enterprise of BrewDog, a non-conformist brewer par excellence. It has reinterpreted the traditional beers and offered new ones, inspired by the Anglo-American school or without any links with the past. The brilliant marketing used to publicize its products or simply to attract attention is sometimes criticized for its excesses (as in the case of the beer called The End of the History with an alcohol content of 55%, sold in bottles contained in stuffed squirrels); but it undoubtedly has a strong media impact. Under its influence the whole of Scotland is rapidly rewriting its own brewing history.

# STRONG SCOTCH ALE

FAMILY: TOP FERMENTATION
CATEGORY: IRISH AND SCOTCH ALE
STYLE: STRONG SCOTCH ALE OR WEE HEAVY
ORIGIN: SCOTLAND

Scotch ales are the typical, traditional Scottish beers. Produced with local ingredients because of the difficulty (and cost) of importing hop from the southernmost regions of the British Isles, these beers are made with barley malts, produced in Scotland, and they are found in most of the pubs in Glasgow and Edinburgh as well as in isolated villages. Scotch ales are divided into four types that differ mainly in their alcoholic content and they are still named today after their original cost, namely 60, 70 and 80 shillings (also known as Scottish Light, Heavy and Export) with an alcohol content of between 2.5 and 5% abv. Finally there is the 90 shilling, commonly known (Strong) Scotch Ale or Wee Heavy, the most alcoholic and expensive.

PRODUCTION

In addition to a generous quantity of Pale malts, the grist also includes Roasted and Crystal malts, more for their color than their sweetness, usually obtained by the caramelization process that takes place during the mashing. Often they also use small amounts of malts smoked with various kinds of wood or with peat. Being of English origin, the use of hops is minimal.

CHARACTERISTICS

The color ranges from amber to that of a monk's habit, with abundant foam tending towards cappuccino. The yeast's esters and alcoholic notes (in the "warmer" versions) are also present in the nose, as are notes of caramel, earth and in some cases, smokiness and peat.

Flavors of prunes, raisins and dried fruit are also detectable. The body varies from medium to full, in some cases even viscous, while the carbonation is moderate. The result is a well-balanced beer, in spite of its sweetness, with a dry finish and burnt notes.

Alcohol content: about 6.5-10% abv.
Pairing: with meat dishes, also lamb and in the case of the peaty versions with blue and well-seasoned cheeses.

# GERMANY

Germany has a very ancient brewing tradition but it has also imposed on the world the modern Pale Lager beers, based on production techniques developed in its industrial breweries. In spite of the Bavarian Purity Law imposed on all the States of the Federation, which remained in force until the end of the 20th century, the country has developed a great variety of types of beers and various exceptions to the Purity Law. This variety can be explained by the region being made up of numerous small principalities, each with its own laws and traditions. So each area and each town has a unique repository of beers with deep historical roots.

In Bavaria we find the legendary wheat beers, the Weissbier (white beers) or Weizenbier (wheat beers) that are characterized by the phenol of the yeast and the rush of wheat malt. There are also beers in the Hell style that could be described as masterpieces of simplicity, more so than the Märzen beers that are drunk in vast quantities during the Oktoberfest held every year in Munich (except during time of war or other catastrophes). This event consists of a sort of amusement park with enormous structures housing the city's breweries and attracting millions of visitors including numerous foreigners.

Traveling slightly further north, we find that the ancient tradition of the Zoigl beers is still very much alive; these are beers produced by a few families that over the centuries have acquired the right to brewing in the town's communal brewery. This beer is then sold directly at the brewer's home, sometimes in the living room transformed into a kind of pub, and sometimes in a special premises set up like a "Gasthaus," a kind of inn or wine bar that also serves food.

Besides Munich, there are other large cities in Germany that have left their own individual mark on beer styles, such as Dortmund with its Dortmunder, the local response to Hell and Pils.

Cologne too has a very strong brewing tradition that could be described as a counter-trend compared to the rest of the country, with a top-fermenting beer, Kölsch, that is pale, clear and with a low alcohol content that can only be produced within the walls of the city. It is consumed directly in the pubs attached to the brewery, often served straight from the barrels, its low carbonation making it easy to serve.

A few miles from Cologne is Düsseldorf which with its Alt, amber-colored beers again top-fermented, attracts and seduces beer enthusiasts. One of the main avenues of the city is lined with traditional breweries that offer only this beer, produced on site, and its more alcoholic winter version. Here too it is possible to eat traditional dishes accompanied by this low-alcohol beer that with its lightly-toasted notes never disappoints.

Not far from Cologne and Dusseldorf, the city of Bonn has responded with the Bonsch beer, a beer that is however much less interesting than the two previous ones: it seems to have tried to distinguish itself from the Cologne beer by producing one that is too simple.

In Berlin and generally in the former East Germany, most of the traditional beers have been threatened by the more commercial beers that are more profitable. Berliner Weiss has survived with difficulty and today it is enjoying a discreet revival thanks the efforts of many foreign brewers who have relaunched it, although in the capital it has always been possible to enjoy these slightly acid beers, perhaps with woodruff syrup or some other fruit syrup to tone down its acidity. Further south, in Leipzig, Gose beers seem to have been rediscovered recently; these are traditional beers produced in the nearby city of Goslar where this very unusual beer is produced with salted water, wheat and coriander; today it is very famous and imitated in many parts of the world.

Franconia, the northernmost part of Bavaria, is perhaps the most fascinating region for a beer enthusiast, where small family brewers make beer following ancient recipes in outbuildings behind their inns. In and around Bamberg, the brewing capital as well as a splendid city, miraculously spared during the bombing raids of the Second World War, there are still a large number of historic breweries that produce local beers, unique of their kind and based on ancient recipes. It was in Bamberg that Rauchbier was born, those smoky beers that have survived here and are copied and admired today throughout the world. In the taverns annexed to these breweries, vast amounts are drunk of whatever beer is available, according to the season: Fasten (Easter beers), Märzen, Bock, Doppelbock but above all Keller Bier, usually not filtered, well matured in the cellar, Land Bier, and Ungespundet (which in fact means "not filtered") are some of the masterpieces created by these brewers, each one so very simple and yet all so very different from each other.

In smaller villages the choice of where to go to drink a beer is limited if there is only one brewery, but even where there are two or more, it is a tradition that families only patronize one of them. The head of the family will have chosen it for himself and for the generations to come. In summer the larger breweries open their Biergarten, open-air pubs, while the smaller brewers sell their beer to independent pubs. Every evening (and often in the afternoon as well) the local inhabitants meet in these places to enjoy the sun and the warmth without giving up their beer.

Germany has a strong tradition of brewing schools, of growing barley and hops and of malting, together forming a complete production chain of the highest quality. While the Purity Law may have restricted the brewers' imagination in their production and the evolution of styles by creating a certain conservatism, it is also true that in recent times something has changed. Besides the classic noble hops, pillars of the Teutonic tradition, new types of hops with fascinating aromatic properties have been introduced, an impressive response by the Old Continent to the continuous flow of innovations from the New World. Also some local brewers have started to use American varieties so as to produce less typical styles, while arousing the interest of a younger public of beer enthusiasts. The good omen is that the new hops grown in the Hallertau (the most important area of cultivation) are better adapted to the types of local beers than those from North America.

# MÜNCHNER HELL

FAMILY: BOTTOM FERMENTATION
CATEGORY: LIGHT LAGER
STYLE: MÜNCHNER HELL
ORIGIN: GERMANY (MUNICH)

Hell beers were born in the Spaten brewery in Munich in the late 19th century to counter the success of the Pils beers of Bohemia that were becoming increasingly widespread and popular. It set out to imitate their pale golden yellow color (obtained by using Pils malt but of German origin) and herbaceous aromas (obtained through the typical native hop). Their distinctive element is that they emphasize more the sweetness of the malt rather than the bitterness of the hop (using half that of a Bohemian Pils).

The German term "Hell" implicitly includes the word "bier" and it simply means a "light beer."

## PRODUCTION

To produce such a simple, clean beer, the brewer must pay close attention to the quality of the raw materials and, perhaps even more than for other bottom-fermenting beers, a low fermentation temperature and long maturation in the cold, to completely avoid the formation of fruity esters.

## CHARACTERISTICS

These are beers with a medium body, mellow and rounded, always well-balanced and never sickly, thanks to the moderate but skilful use of the hops that discreetly support and accompany the maltiness.

It is an "old girl-friend" calling you, a great classic to whom you cannot say no.

Alcohol content: about 4.7-5.4%.

Pairing: it is perfect beer to accompany light dishes but it can also stand up to the heat of spicy curried sausage.

# MÜNCHNER DUNKEL

FAMILY: BOTTOM FERMENTATION
CATEGORY: DARK LAGER
STYLE: MÜNCHNER DUNKEL
ORIGIN: SOUTHERN GERMANY

These dark Lagers, today much less widespread and less famous than their modern little granddaughters, the Münchner Hell, are in fact the original beers, those that were stored in the coolness of caves since the 1500s. It is very likely that they used the naturally selected bottom-fermenting yeast that was then isolated by Hansen. They are the original beers of southern Bavaria, historically with low hop levels because the region is far from the center of the hop trade (the northern cities of the Hanseatic League) and because of their use of "gruit."
In German "Dunkel" means "dark."

## PRODUCTION
It is traditionally produced with 100% Munich malt and a long decoction that, because of the caramelization of the sugars, further emphasizes the color and taste of this malt.

## CHARACTERISTICS
With their distinctive brown/garnet-red color and dense creamy-colored foam, they have a rich fragrance, typical of the amber-colored malt of Munich with its notes of caramel and bread crusts. Their body is almost always generous without being heavy and the sweetness and complexity of malts still prevails with only a hint of toast and noble hops.
If you go to Bavaria, try and find some that are not filtered, produced by small artisanal brewers… a journey back in time! And do not be put off by the color!

Alcohol content: about 4.5-5.6% abv.
Pairing: grilled salamella (sausage).

# MÄRZEN/OKTOBERFEST

FAMILY: BOTTOM FERMENTATION
CATEGORY: EUROPEAN AMBER LAGER
STYLE: MÄRZEN/OKTOBERFEST
ORIGIN: GERMANY (MUNICH)

Before the invention of refrigerators, the month of March (Märzen in German) was the last month that beer could be made because of the rising temperatures of spring and summer. Excessive warmth prevented good beers being made both because of the thermal stress under which the yeast had to work and the proliferation of bacteria that damaged the beer. Although beer-makers in late medieval times had no knowledge of microbiology, they were aware that they had to recreate autumn and winter conditions when beers made during that period were the best. As a result they began using caves carved out of the rock as storage place for the ice that they had accumulated during the winter together with as much beer as possible. So March became a month of very hard work: the objective was to "store" the beer for the summer but also to use up all the remaining hops and malt before the new harvest and the start of the new season's production. Märzen beers were particularly good for keeping in this way because they were very rich in malt, thus having a slightly higher alcohol content, as well as a generous taste of hops, both fundamental elements to increase their shelf-life.

But when production started again in October it was necessary to have all the barrels available, so they had to be emptied. And what better solution than a village party? Compared to those beers drunk in the first warm months of the year, these end-of-season beers, matured for several months, tended to have a stronger malt taste while with the passing of time both the bitterness and the fresh hop aromas had faded.

This plausible story provides a reasonable explanation for the strong malt taste and the robustness of the Märzen beers as well as the ancient origins of the Oktoberfest.

But the reason for the institutionalization of the modern Oktoberfest was the wedding of Prince Ludwig and Princess Therese of Saxony that took place in Munich on October 12, 1810. An open space at the edge of the city was made available for the inhabitants so that they too could take part in the festivities. Known since then as Theresienwiese, this area is where the biggest beer festival in the world takes place: the largest both in terms of the number of visitors and the quantity of beer sold. It is a wonderful opportunity for the six leading brewers in Munich, who are the only ones allowed to set up their gigantic stands and dispense beer.

CHARACTERISTICS

With an orangey, reddish-gold color, it is one of the classiest malted styles: mellow, complex and elegant.

The March beer must be drunk in October: long live the one-liter tankard! (A liter is a US quart.)

Alcohol content: about 4.8-5.7% abv.
Pairing: shin and pretzel or roast pork with sauce chasseur and boiled potato dumplings.

# SCHWARZBIER

FAMILY: BOTTOM FERMENTATION
CATEGORY: DARK LAGER
STYLE: SCHWARZBIER
ORIGIN: GERMANY

Schwarzbier literally means "black beer," sometimes also called black Pils (although having none of the bitterness of the Pils) but it is hard to find examples that are truly black and opaque (except if you use a very wide glass). They are however the darkest of the Lagers, even though they have a much less intense and challenging profile than one would think at first glance.

Of uncertain origin, according to some they were developed in the wake of the successful English Porter beers, while others believe they are a variant of the Münchner Dunkel.

CHARACTERISTICS

This beer looks very elegant with its dark brown color with ruby-colored and brilliant brick-red reflections, combined with an abundant foam the color of cappuccino. Its aroma is surprisingly delicate with notes of roast coffee, perfectly balanced by the malted notes, and no traces of fruity esters. The taste is never pungent or acrid, burnt or bitter: coffee, chocolate, vanilla and the usual German non-invasive sweetness is accompanied by a hop flavor that is rather discreet, both as far as bitterness and aroma are concerned, but which reveals itself in the finish that tends towards dryness without actually being so.

With a medium-light body, good carbonation and a modest alcohol content, it is a very approachable dark beer.

Trying a good Schwarzbier will be a revelation: it will completely remove any prejudice you may have regarding Lagers and black beers.

Alcohol content: about 4.4-5.4% abv.

Pairing: grilled salmon trout, particularly those found at the Annafest in Forchheim at the end of July.

# TRADITIONAL BOCK

FAMILY: BOTTOM FERMENTATION
CATEGORY: BOCK
STYLE: TRADITIONAL BOCK
ORIGIN: GERMANY

These beers owe their name to their city of origin, Heinbeck in Lower Saxony, that was already an important center of trade and of beer production in the time of the Hanseatic League. The name "Bock" came much later when these beers spread to the far south of Germany, to Bavaria where in the local dialect the name Heinbeck became "Bock," a word that also has another meaning, "goat," an image that often adorns the labels of these beers.

## PRODUCTION
This beer, full of character, is a true celebration of the amber-colored malts, such as Munich and Vienna, that have here found one of their most beautiful expressions. The continental hops are used very sparingly, just slightly to mitigate the malted sweetness that always marks the finish of a Bock.

## CHARACTERISTICS
Typically brown in the past, today there are also versions tending towards amber and copper, but they are always brilliant after long ageing and with a fine, compact, persistent foam. The richness and complexity of the full-bodied malt and the softness of the drink are felt by both the nose and the mouth, and the beer is never mundane because of the alcohol that begins to be felt.

Alcohol content: about 6.3-7.2% abv.
Pairing: smoked meat carpaccio.

In the Bock family there is also to be found the clearer dry-hopped Maibock; the more challenging elder sisters Doppelbock (with an alcohol content of up to 10%) and the extreme Eisbock: this can reach very high alcohol levels due to a particular stage of the production process that involves freezing it and removing a percentage of the water from the beer, which thus becomes "concentrated."

# KÖLSCH

FAMILY: TOP FERMENTATION
CATEGORY: LIGHT HYBRID BEER
STYLE: KÖLSCH
ORIGIN: GERMANY (COLOGNE)

This is the typical beer of Cologne (in German Köln, hence Kölsch) and one of the few beers with a protected designation of origin. After the Second World War the producers of the city joined together to form the Kölsch Konvention to protect their product by drawing up simple production rules and defining the style of their beer. It must be pale and brilliant (in other words, filtered), top-fermented, with hop flavors, well-rounded with a light body, and most important of all, made in Cologne. The Kölsch beers were derived in the 19th century from the brown Altbier, more or less in the same way as in England Pale Ale was derived from Brown Ale, thanks to the availability of the modern light-colored malts that were the result of the scientific and industrial revolutions of that time.

## PRODUCTION

It is produced with a characteristic top-fermenting yeast, but with the temperatures kept as low as possible so as not to emphasize its fruity profile too much, although this is one of its trade marks. The beer is then left to mature in a cold place in the same way as the Lagers but for a shorter time. It is for this reason that Kölsch is classed in the category of hybrid beers.

It is one of the palest beers in Germany with a white but not too persistent foam and a subtle, faint and delicate aroma of fruit (apple) and hop. The taste is also extremely well balanced with a dry finish but not excessively bitter. An inexperienced taster might actually mistake it for a Pale Lager or even a light Golden Ale.

It is a real "session beer," very refreshing and never boring.

Alcohol volume: about 4.4-5.2% abv.
Pairing: light dishes such as chicken salad or the classic Bratwurst.

# BERLINER WEISSE

FAMILY: TOP FERMENTATION
CATEGORY: SOUR ALE
STYLE: BERLINER WEISSE
ORIGIN: GERMANY (BERLIN)

An absolutely unique and atypical beer, it is hard to find far from its place of origin and even in Berlin where it is only produced by small independent brewers and brew-pubs and by a large group that owns two very famous labels. It is another rare case of beer with a protected designation of origin.

## PRODUCTION

This beer is multi-faceted and enigmatic in its originality. It is to all intents and purposes a Weiss because it is made with a large percentage of wheat malt, but it has none of the typical features of the Bavarian Weizen: only a light flavor of wheat and an exuberant carbonation. It is certainly a top-fermenting beer because of the *Saccharomyces cerevisiae* yeast used but it is also inoculated with a *Lactobacillus* (of the Delbrucki type) that gives the beer its acidity and sharpness, reminiscent of the Lambic beers with spontaneous fermentation. There is no doubt that it is a tart beer and extremely pale, but there is a tradition of serving it diluted with sweet fruit syrups (woodruff and raspberry) that also have a strong coloring effect.

## CHARACTERISTICS

The color in the undiluted version is a very pale straw yellow, sometimes opalescent and with an abundant but short-lived foam, while the aroma is undoubtedly dominated by slightly acid notes; the very perceptive may find delicate fruity and floral tones.

Sharp, fresh and light, both in body and alcohol, it is deliberately made to quench the thirst with its dry finish and absence of sweetness.

Alcohol content: about 2.8-3.8% abv.
Pairing: its acidity, pungency and elegance, like Champagne, make it a perfect aperitif.

# WEIZENBIER (WEISSBIER)

FAMILY: TOP FERMENTATION
CATEGORY: GERMAN WHEAT AND RYE BEER
STYLE: WEIZENBIER (WEISSBIER)
ORIGIN: GERMANY (MUNICH)

It is the nth style created by the Bavarian brewers, today very widespread and popular with the general public, distinguished by its large amount of wheat malt, not below 50%. For these beers brewers use special top-fermenting yeasts that are responsible, together with the wheat, for the typical spicy clove and ripe banana aroma with phenolic and slightly citric accents. But one must watch out for the name under which they are marketed. This may be Weiss (white) that refers to the color, although in reality they are pale yellow, or it may be Weizen (wheat) that refers to its main ingredient, wheat malt. In addition to the generic names Weiss and Weizen, it is sometimes marketed under other names that refer more to its characteristics. "Kristall" tells us that the beer has been filtered and not re-fermented to appear sparkling. Hefeweizen, that is Weizen with yeast (Hefe=yeast), is the name given to the non-filtered versions that are re-fermented and very opalescent with a deeper color. These are also the most widespread.

Finally there are other Weizen beers that do not belong to this style: the Dunkel Weizen, so called because of their dark color (Dunkel=dark), in which the fruity aromas have been replaced by those of roast coffee and liquorish. There are also Weizenbock and the Weizen Doppel-Bock, dark wheat beers that share the very complex character and high alcohol content typical of Bock and Doppel-Bock.

These are very straightforward and popular beers, very approachable. They are sometimes unfairly snubbed by self-styled experts who have maybe forgotten that it survived the notorious Purity Law because the royal family of Bavaria owned the exclusive production rights.

Many enjoy it with a slice of lemon elegantly placed on the rim of the glass. But who are we to say… "de gustibus non est disputandum" ("in matters of taste there is no argument"). Try it both ways and then you can decide how you prefer it.

Alcohol content: about 4.3-5.6% abv.
Pairing: in Munich you can enjoy it with white Vienna sausage and sweet mustard as a mid-morning snack.

# GOSE

FAMILY: TOP FERMENTATION (HYBRID)
CATEGORY: CURRENTLY BEING DEFINED
STYLE: GOSE
ORIGIN: GERMANY (GOSLAR AND LEIPZIG)

Today Gose is identified as the beer of Leipzig, the city that has adopted and revived it. But in reality this beer has its origins in the town of Goslar, built along the banks of the river Gose. Around the year 1000 it began to prosper thanks to the discovery of silver and copper deposits and its famous beer production. The brewers used water that were extremely salty (probably because of the vast amounts of minerals in the subsoil) that gave this beer its unique characteristic, that of being salted.

With the decline of the mines in the early Middle Ages, the town experienced serious depopulation and many brewers of Gose beer had to seek their fortune elsewhere. Some settled in the larger city of Leipzig where their salted beer was much appreciated and it became increasingly popular as time went by, so much so that at the beginning of the 20th century, it had become the most widespread beer. The success of Gose in Leipzig was such that it seriously undermined the economic sustainability of the Goslar brewers so that the production of Gose was prohibited by the local council. After the Second World War, in the then German Democratic Republic or East Germany, Gose beer suffered a serious decline. It was only in the late 1980s that it was revived by a beer enthusiast who was determined to serve this beer in his pub, a former Gosen tavern that he was renovating. The revived Gose did not arouse much interest among the neighboring brewers, so this beer enthusiast had to go to a Berlin-based brewer for his production. Even now there are still very few producers but the enthusiasm and popularity generated by this "strange" beer among those who try it is unparalleled.

## PRODUCTION

It is one of the most original beers in the world: it is made with salt and therefore it is salty; it is made with a large amount of wheat malt and is therefore defined as a Weiss beer; it is flavored with coriander as well as the hops and it is therefore spicy; and it is fermented with top-fermenting yeast but lactic bacteria are also added, so it is therefore a sharp beer with a hybrid fermentation.

## CHARACTERISTICS

The beer is golden and transparent with a rich, white, very persistent foam; it has a light-medium body, a delicate aroma but one that hints at the beer's spicy and sharp nature that are both dominant on the palate, together with its surprising salty taste that may amaze but is always appreciated. Fresh, dry, refreshing and thirst-quenching.

Alcohol content: about 4.5-5% abv.
Pairing: seafood.

# CZECH REPUBLIC

In the Czech Republic beer drinkers are many and… committed: it is estimated that the annual consumption per capita is about 45 US gallons (170 liters). Comparing this figure to the US one, which is about 18 gallons (70 liters), you will see that the art of brewing is an integral part of everyday life.

Unlike the landscape of Bavaria and Franconia, where the local pub is attached to the brewery, Bohemia is also dotted with clubs, bars, cafes and pubs where the Czechs do not stop at the first glass. But there are still breweries where you can consume on the spot, including the most historic breweries, those that survived the years of the Iron Curtain. In many cases these are part of large groups, as in the case of Pilsner Urquell, now owned by the South African company SAB Miller (which also owns Peroni and Nastro Azzurro). In the historic area of Pilsen it is possible to enjoy the delicious unfiltered, unpasteurized Pils that is still produced nearby.

Historically, the beers are bottom-fermented, but Pils was introduced fairly recently, in the mid-19th century. The most traditional beers have a color ranging from golden yellow to dark amber, hints of Roasted malts, and a low alcohol content. As well as its relatively low price, this explains the incredible consumption. The simplicity of the beer's production is matched by the ease of drinking it: one really pulls the other. At U Flekù in the center of Prague you can drink more than one beer first made in 1499 that has survived to our day, a very pleasant Dunkel (literally, in German, "dark") of 4.6% abv. With modern production techniques it has definitely changed, but it retains all its appeal and its charm, especially if consumed inside the restaurant in front of the brewery that emanates a history of over five hundred years.

A tip. In Prague and its surroundings alcohol content is not always expressed as alcohol by volume (e.g. 5% abv). Most of the time it is given in degrees Plato, so a beer of 13° does not mean a strongly alcoholic beer, since it represents an alcoholic content of about 4.5% abv.

# BOHEMIAN PILSNER

FAMILY: BOTTOM FERMENTATION
CATEGORY: PILSNER
STYLE: BOHEMIAN PILSNER
ORIGIN: CZECH REPUBLIC

The archetype of pale hopped beer. Pilsen? Pilsener? Pilsner? Pils? All these names refer to the Bohemian city of Plzeň (Pilsen in German) where this magnificent beer saw the light. It was created by the Josef Groll, a "modern" German brewer who had been specially asked to come over from Bavaria where he had already started using the new knowledge and technology of the industrial revolution to obtain pale, clear beers: bottom-fermenting yeast, strict control of the malting process, and the use of thermometers and refrigerators. Josef made a very simple choice: to combine his know-how with the raw materials of the region: the aromatic noble hop of Zatec (Saaz), the famous malt of Moravia and the very sweet water of Plzeň.

The result was a beer with an extraordinary golden color that revolutionized the history of this beer, which until then had been red-brown, brown or dark. Imagine then how much the invention of drinking glasses contributed to bringing out the beauty of its color.

It is a beer that should be looked at closely because the market, saturated with this type of beer, offers both sublime creations and shameful, characterless interpretations. Unfortunately, today anyone can produce this beer anywhere and use the names Pils, Pilsner or Pilsener because they were not registered at the time. You will recognize the original beer by the adjective "Urquell."

## PRODUCTION

Made with bottom-fermenting yeast, Pils malts, noble hops and soft water, it is ideally brewed through multiple decoction (but nowadays through multi-step infusion), followed by long maturation in cold conditions.

## CHARACTERISTICS

A pale golden color, it is also limpid and bright, even in the artisanal versions, with a fine-grained white foam that is abundant and long-lasting. It has a delicate but complex aroma with herbaceous and floral notes.
Pils are among the most bitter of the Lagers, but it is an elegant bitterness, never biting, that must always be counterbalanced by the body and the malts. It is a beer that is more based on the balance and harmony of the aromatic and gustatory sensations than on its "muscles" or on any individual detail.

Alcohol content: about 4.5-5.4% abv.
Pairing: slices of veal marinated in lemon and served with oil and arugula.

# AUSTRIA

Austria has written an important chapter in the history of beer. It is called "Vienna," like its capital, and it is an amber-colored malt much appreciated for its color, its delicate flavor and its mellowness. It is one of the most frequently used malts, together with the Pilsner, Pale and Munich malts. In the mid-19th century the Viennese entrepreneurial brewer Anton Dreher created a beer style that is still known as "Vienna," an amber-colored Lager with its very own personality, different from its German cousins that are obviously also to be found in large quantities in Austria too.

Thanks to this beer Dreher succeeded in greatly increasing his production, even conquering the market in Italy, especially in the border regions that passed from the Austrian Empire to the new Italian nation at that historic moment in time, and for many years the Vienna style remained one of the most popular. In addition to the historical events involving Austria in Mexico, ruled for a short time by the Habsburg Maximilian I, the Vienna beers also made their way to that Central American country where they are still produced and successfully marketed by local brands, although using regional recipes and materials that are not the same as the originals.

Today with the standardization of tastes and production, especially where Lagers are concerned, the Vienna-style beers are in danger of disappearing and again we owe their rediscovery and revival to a network of small artisanal brewers who, concentrating on quality, have revived and relaunched so many forgotten styles.

But Vienna beers continue to attract large number of enthusiasts in the traditional Stube (those places with the stove well in view, to warm up those around it) and they are a perfect pairing with the local cuisine. A few innovations are beginning to be introduced, such as the use of new types of hop imported from across the Atlantic, and more modern styles that are only found in a few brew-pubs that are trying hard to survive economically, carving themselves a small slice of the market. Another great innovation for the Austrian beer world came from the abbey of Stift Engelszell (Engelshartzell) where in silence and complying with the rules of the Trappist monks (the abbey is in fact part of the Cistercian Order of the Strict Observance) the Gregorius beer was born, a beer that is well worth getting to know better. Inspired by Belgian beer, it is very alcoholic, thus breaking with local traditions but not with monastic ones. Because the production of these beers, like that of the liqueurs, follows Trappist precepts, the bottles can bear the hexagonal label "Authentic Trappist Product.".

# VIENNA LAGER

FAMILY: BOTTOM FERMENTATION
CATEGORY: EUROPEAN AMBER LAGER
STYLE: VIENNA LAGER
ORIGIN: AUSTRIA

This style has its roots in that of the old Märzen beers and its history is closely interwoven with the evolution of the technology applied to beer-making. Anton Dreher, a Viennese Austrian, and Gabriel Sedlmayr, a German from Munich, were two enterprising brewers, friends and rivals who were trying to "lighten" the color of Märzen beers by using new lighter malts, even amber-colored ones that were then called Vienna. Dreher was the more daring and he made a decidedly lighter beer, although not as blond as Pils. From Sedlmayr, who was already using it, he borrowed the new low-fermentation yeast that had only just been isolated in a pure form.

This is how the Vienna beers were born in Austria as a style in their own right, while in Munich the beers lightened and fermented in this way were called "Viennese-style Märzen." It is interesting to note that in Germany, a couple of decades ago, the Viennese-style Märzen was displaced by a slightly darker version, made with another new malt called Munich, and this subsequently became known as Oktoberfest because it was presented for the first time at the famous Bavarian beer festival.

CHARACTERISTICS

Getting back to our style: amber-copper in color with a persistent white foam, the Vienna beers perfectly express the richness and elegance of the malt, both in their aromas and their flavors. The hop emerges only at the end to balance and absorb the sweetness in a finish that never gets boring.

A beer at risk of extinction: let us save it by drinking it!

Alcohol content: about 4.5-5.5 % abv.
Pairing: with a tomato, mozzarella and sausage pizza.

# UNITED STATES

This country has played a decisive role since the 1970s in reviving the enthusiasm for beer ("The Modern Renaissance").

Its secret has been the passion, the work and the sacrifices of individuals rather than companies. All the new generation of brewers have done more than just "putting on a face" by bringing to the fore beer as a product made by an individual, and not by anonymous, distant mega-companies that base everything on marketing. The decision of what kind of beer to make and how to make it has come back to the brewer, with his feelings and his skills, and is not decided by a market research department that seeks to understand what kind of people want to drink beer, or even worse, by accountants who only want to produce beer at the lowest possible cost, regardless of what the outcome will be.

Small brewers improvising with simple equipment and few economic resources, often with experience of home brewing, started to make beers that were a bit different from the usual (but not too much, because of the few standard raw materials available). They persuaded people to taste their beers, trying to win their trust and slowly carving out a small local market. They tried to make people understand the difference between the beers they were making and those on supermarket shelves. They invited people to visit their facilities; they devised festivals, parties, workshops and initiatives of every kind and type; they taught those who were interested to make beer at home. They created effective slogans such as "Support your local Brewery" that appealed to hardcore enthusiasts but also to newcomers. They knew how to work together, helping each other to improve their beers and exchanging tips. They made collective purchases of raw materials: first spontaneously and then formally through an association that looked after their interests. The common goal was to identify and recognize their product, "craft beers," and to distinguish them from industrial ones.

The vastness of the country, the high per capita consumption and the ease with which their products were distinguishable from the bland beers of large retailers, were elements that prevented the onset of the fear of competition, and indeed favored this kind of "fraternal spirit" that was, in addition to the quality of the beers, the basis of their very great success.

Meanwhile the question "What is a craft beer" and how it is defined or standardized is always open to debate. In the US, as in many other countries, what the public is looking for in these beers is now established: quality, sensation, emotion, surprise, satisfaction, and curiosity. And U.S. brewers understood this immediately.

They started with the huge variety of historic styles of European brewing traditions (especially the English and Belgian, and to a lesser extent German), and this in itself was enough to amaze the American public. Then they started to interpret these styles more or less creatively, so that today many classic styles exist in variations with the significant addition of the adjective "American" (American Lager, American Barley Wine, American IPA, etc.).

THE MAJOR COUNTRIES AND THE MAJOR STYLES OF BEER

The most revolutionary weapon that has been used is that of research into raw materials, and in particular into the one most neglected by industrial brewers, hops. Many new types of hops have become available, with really amazing flavor profiles that were unimaginable just a few years ago: all those with citrus notes of grapefruit, pink grapefruit, mandarin, and the more balsamic aromas, described as "piney" and "resinous."

In addition to the new possibilities of aromatic hops, Americans micro-breweries have also dared to tackle even the more difficult bitter side, elevating the thresholds that are normal in many styles provocatively and even excessively. The bitter taste is difficult, since acid tastes are not "natural" for the human body that, ancestrally, associates them with danger or toxicity (poisons, decay, etc.). These are "acquired" tastes, not like sweet and salty tastes that are spontaneous. Only those who have learned to enjoy an espresso coffee without sugar can fully appreciate this and explain why they will not go back to sweetening it. The same is true of the "new world" of bitter beers, a "new world" that awaits you with open arms with a thousand choices and variations. Put yourself in the hands of a good publican and let yourself be guided: the path is long but pleasant and surprising.

Certainly the phenomenon of ultra-hoppy beers is justified by the effect of historical twists and turns, but as the past has already shown, it could take very little to get us back to a world of sweet beers. What do you think would happen if today's tax system based on the alcohol content of a beer, on the principle of "the stronger it is, the more you must pay," was changed to a system of taxation on the degree of bitterness, on the principle of "the more bitter a beer is, the more you must pay"?

Posterity will be the judge…

# AMERICAN PALE ALE (APA)

FAMILY: TOP FERMENTATION
CATEGORY: AMERICAN ALE
STYLE: AMERICAN PALE ALE (APA)
ORIGIN: UNITED STATES

American Pale Ales, commonly known as APA, are an American re-edition of the English Pale Ales using local ingredients. The hops, originally from Europe, transplanted in America and then crossed with new selections, greatly influenced first the world of American brewing, then the rest of the world. APA beers marked a historic break with tradition with their low alcohol content, their new fragrances, their new flavors and their discreet bitterness. They started a revolution that is still ongoing and it has led to the birth of many new styles of beer such as American IPA, Double IPA, Imperial IPA and numerous re-interpretations that are emerging throughout the world.

## PRODUCTION

Top-fermentation is used and the main ingredients are Pale malt produced in America, some malt for sweetness, sometimes Roasted, and above all hops, in particular those exuding fragrances of citrus. The hops are added mainly in late-hopping (in the final stages of mashing the wort) and often also in dry-hopping (during the maturation stage of the beer), precisely to enhance the aromatic character of this type.

## CHARACTERISTICS

The color can vary enormously, from hazy-amber to a deep amber, depending on the malts used, while the foam is white, creamy and persistent.

The fragrances of the American hops dominate the malts with citrus, resinous and herbaceous notes. The body is light and the carbonation moderately high, and if the hopping is excessive, an unwelcome astringency may be perceived. The sweet, roasted or toasted flavors of the malts are overpowered by the bitterness while at the same time balancing them. The citrus and resinous notes of the hops reemerge in the long aftertaste.

Alcohol content: 4.5-6.2% abv.

Pairing: these are thirst-quenching beers that can be drunk at all times of the day and perfect as aperitif, thanks to their low alcohol content and refreshing effect.

# STANDARD AMERICAN LAGER

FAMILY: BOTTOM FERMENTATION
CATEGORY: LIGHT LAGER
STYLE: STANDARD AMERICAN LAGER
ORIGIN: UNITED STATES

This is in fact an international style that includes all the normal Pale Lagers commonly sold on the mass-market.

Given that it involves the use of large amounts of cereals such as corn and rice, ingredients used in America to make beer since time immemorial, it is included in this section on the United States.

Usually the inexpensive cereals, corn and rice are not used together, but sometimes in very cheap beers both are used, accompanied by another very cheap ingredient: sugar. Laws that vary from country to country have imposed limits on these additions that might otherwise reach very high levels.

The "craft beer" movement did not want to improve or dignify the style of Lager, nor did it have the possibility of doing so. Perhaps it was a strategic choice, influenced by the desire to set itself apart unequivocally from a product intended for the mass market by producing a completely different product. But it is also true that Lagers, with their long period of cold maturation, take longer to produce and therefore need a larger number storage tanks, greater financial investment and larger warehouses that could be too expensive for many artisanal micro-breweries.

CHARACTERISTICS

These are very pale beers with a white evanescent foam, with weak fragrances of malt, maize and hops. The taste is refreshing, the body is light, and the finish is dry and short-lived because of the extreme fizziness that prickles the tongue.

It is one of those beers that should be drunk iced, even from the bottle, without thinking too much about it.

Alcohol content: about 4.2-5.3% abv.

Pairing: its blandness does not lend itself to gastronomic pairings but it would be perfect with a hot-dog.

# IMPERIAL IPA

FAMILY: TOP FERMENTATION
CATEGORY: INDIA PALE ALE (IPA)
STYLE: IMPERIAL IPA
ORIGIN: UNITED STATES

Imperial IPA is a style developed fairly recently to give a classification to all the extreme versions of American IPA that have labels with adjectives such as "double," "extra" or "extreme" IPA. The need of American brewers to create something new and then take it to the extreme has focused mainly on the hops, truly enormous quantities being used in every stage of the production where it is possible to do so. In some cases special equipment has been invented to make the most of the aromatic properties of hops. Today brewers in other countries are following the example of Imperial IPA in their use of hops.

## PRODUCTION

The malts play a fundamental role in contrasting with the bitterness of the hops. They may be American, English or German and are used as an aroma at various stages, from the mashing, in the whirlpool, up to the maturation and in a complex medley, worthy of an alchemist. The top-fermenting yeast is usually neutral so it is not expected to release esters but to work on producing alcohol until attenuation.

## CHARACTERISTICS

The color ranges from intense golden to copper-colored while the foam is fine-grained and persistent.
Hops dominate the nose, forming a complex amalgam of fragrances, from citrus to floral and fruity as well as herbaceous and resinous.
The malt, with its sweetness, creates a contrast with the bitterness that otherwise would be excessive, partly balancing the beer that nonetheless has a long and perceptible bitterness. The body is medium, the carbonation is medium-high and a not-excessive dryness contributes to its drinkability, leaving a mellow sensation of alcohol. The finish is long and intense, dominated by bitter notes of citrus fruit. In some cases it could be considered a meditation beer with balsamic notes.

Alcohol content: between 7.5 and 10% abv.

# AMERICAN IPA

FAMILY: TOP FERMENTATION
CATEGORY: INDIA PALE ALE (IPA)
STYLE: AMERICAN IPA
ORIGIN: UNITED STATES

American India Pale Ales are an interpretation of the English IPA by the micro-breweries in the United States. They differ from the original India Pale Ales in their use of local ingredients and especially at the "hand" of the brewers, generous in their use of hops, mostly from the north-west coast, in pursuit of new flavors and a more perceptible bitterness. Many use hop varieties of the 4 Cs (Cascade. Columbus, Centennial, Chinook), but other varieties such as Amarillo, Willamette and more recently Citra and Simcoe are now used in IPA, in particular along the West Coast of California where instead of the gold rush we are now seeing the "rush for hops." And the IPA beers are a more alcoholic and more hoppy version of the American Pale Ales.

## PRODUCTION
The Pale malts form the basis of the grist to which Caramel malts are added, and in some cases also roasted hops. Hops are also used in large amounts in all the phases of the mashing, to enhance the bitterness and the aroma. The technique of dry-hopping, the addition of generous amounts of hops to enhance the aroma of the beer, is much used. The yeasts are usually neutral so they do no produce esters but are involved in the attenuation (dryness).

## CHARACTERISTICS
The color ranges from golden to hazy amber-colored, in some cases with orange reflections and usually clear, with a white, fine-grained, persistent foam.
They immediately strike one with their intense fragrance of hops, lemony, resinous, floral and fruity, that overpower the subtle notes of Caramel malts. Mellow to the palate, the body is medium to light and the carbonation medium-high. Again the hops dominate in the mouth but the malt (with caramel notes and at times also roasted) balances the bitterness that, although perceptible, is very tolerable. The long-lasting aftertaste explodes with hoppy notes, that are already perceptible in the nose.

Alcohol content: 5.5-7.5% abv.
Pairing: they are perfect to accompany barbecues: grilled meat and sausages.

# CASCADIAN DARK ALE

FAMILY: TOP FERMENTATION
CATEGORY: INDIA PALE ALE (IPA)
STYLE: CASCADIAN DARK ALE OR BLACK IPA
ORIGIN: UNNITED STATES

This is another innovation in the world of American brewing that is now an officially recognized style, as dark as a Stout but as hoppy as an IPA.

Cascadian Dark Ales were born in the north-west of the United States, between the Cascade Range and the valleys of Yakima and Willamette. It is an agricultural region where barley for beer production is cultivated, but most importantly most of the hops in the US are grown there. So it is the major production center for many of the modern aromatic hops, the main players in this style.

Several brewers in the region have started producing dark version of their very hoppy beers, at first only for festivals and special events, but very soon their success with the public has led these brewers to include them in their regular production. It was not long before other brewers followed suit, hence the need to identify the new style that someone, to avoid "regionalization," preferred to call Black IPA.

## CHARACTERISTICS

Its distinctive feature is that this is a very dark beer, between dark brown and black, but without the strong and intense flavors and fragrances of roast malt: the malts used are dark, with their bitterness removed, or naturally colored malt extracts and, at a blind tasting, it would be difficult to detect its presence because its main contribution is to the color.

In addition this beer must have a strong hoppy character, typical of an IPA, with the lemony, spicy, resinous and floral aromas of the hops of that region (Cascade, Amarillo, Simcoe, Columbus, Centennial, Chinook) that dominate both fragrance and flavor. The finish is decidedly dry and bitter while the body is medium-light. Usually "neutral" yeasts are used, therefore without the production of esters, in order to enhance the aroma of the hops.

One of the surprises of these beers is the interaction of the dark malts with some of the hops, producing fragrances reminiscent of mint and rosemary.

Alcohol content: about 6-8% abv.
Pairing: raw fish and sushi.

# AMERICAN BARLEY WINE

FAMILY: TOP FERMENTATION
CATEGORY: STRONG ALE
STYLE: AMERICAN BARLEY WINE
ORIGIN: UNITED STATES

English Barley Wine was the strongest inspiration for this new style from American micro-breweries that stands out for the greater role played by hops: the bitterness is very intense even though the aroma is elegant and rich with citrus and balsamic notes.

The austerity of the English versions leaves room for the imagination, inspiration, and the desire to "go further" of contemporary brewers who, in this style, compete a little to see who can makes it stronger, richer and more opulent.

CHARACTERISTICS

It has a very intense amber-red (almost never brown) and with a fine foam that is very variable in quantity and duration.

The aroma is a triumph of sensations arising from the abundance of malt and hops, with added ethyl notes and fruity esters produced during fermentation.

The taste is rich and full as is the accompanying body: in these beers sweetness and bitterness are two solid parallel tracks, held together by the alcohol content, but in the end it is the hops that travel further and dominate the long finish.

It is very interesting to do a vertical tasting of young and very mature examples so as to understand its potential for development over time.

Tasting these beers, you may be tempted to consider them mere academic exaggerations but the better-balanced examples can arouse unique emotions.

Alcohol content: about 8-13% abv.

Pairing: while usually being a beer to drink after a meal, more aromatic version of Barley Wine can also be very interesting as a pairing with complex desserts.

# ITALY

The peninsula of Italy has a long brewing tradition. At one time most cities had one or more breweries that produced cold beers that would be consumed during the hotter months. They were seen as summer drinks, the younger sister of wine, but to some extent they were consumed with meals and in taverns, even in winter and even between meals. In the course of the 20th century decline slowly set in, so that virtually none of this remained: most of the breweries closed, leaving no memories of the beers produced. Some other breweries were acquired by large industrial groups. These sometimes kept the name alive (this is the case, for example, with Peroni Nastro Azzurro, Moretti, Ichnusa and Angelo Poretti). Others did away with all traces of the former brand. After a long period of partnership, Forst has acquired Menabrea of Biella in Piedmont, while still leaving it considerable autonomy.

The situation in the early 1990s was really distressing to look at: only the industrial breweries were still active, there were no local ones and consumption was dropping. Only in a very few pubs was it possible to drink a few imported beers that were a little unusual and interesting compared to the industrial lagers that were flat in flavor and fragrance. But by the end of the 1990s things changed and some small (or to tell the truth, microscopic) craft breweries began to open. It was the beginning of the Italian Renaissance: the movement started with a few pioneers and grew exponentially so that now it is hard to keep track of new openings, but it is estimated that there are more than 600 breweries in the country.

Even today in Italy, beer is seen by the majority of the population as a drink to be consumed between meals, refreshing, but without great dignity. Paradoxically, it is in other countries that Italian brewers have been most successful: in about 18 years, Italy has earned itself a position and a reputation in the world of traditional brewing. Other countries watched this first with astonishment, then with curiosity, and today with interest. After the United States it is Italy that is giving a new impetus to the art of brewing.

Italy first followed the traditions of Anglo-Saxon, German and Belgian brewing, then those of North America, sometimes copying existing styles and sometimes re-interpreting them. Often they have left their mark, as in the case of some beers inspired by Kölsch, Pils or Keller of the German school, that have found new life thanks to Italian brewers. Looking at its own territory, Italy has created new types of beer, for example using chestnuts, in which this distinctive ingredient is used raw, boiled, minced, roasted, or as flour.

Recently many breweries have made beers closely linked to their terroir. Because it is difficult to grow hops in Italy, and trying to do so is time consuming and very expensive, there are very few examples of beers using native hops. But local cereals, barley malt and especially indigenous spices and fruits grown in the vicinity of the brewery are commonly used.

Meanwhile, many newly opened or converted pubs sell beers "made in Italy" and some restaurants are starting to supplement the wine list with a beer list, as well as offering some dishes cooked with beer. In short, beer is no longer the little sister of wine, but a product of equal dignity, worthy even of highly reputed starred restaurants.

Italian brewers in their turn have begun to look at the world of wine for inspiration. Italy is a country with a great wine culture that also affects brewers, who adapt to the local situation. Most of the breweries are located in wine regions or they have a brewer who is a friend of some grower, so many beers have come into being that are a connecting link between the worlds of brewing and of wine. As is the local custom, each brewer follows his own path, either using the grapes directly, or the juice, or the wort, or the cooked grape wort, or even marc, to achieve the desired result.

Some even use the traditional Champagne method, complete with riddling, disgorgement and topping up with liqueur d'expedition (a solution of sugar in wine). Each of these beers carries within it not only the character given by the fruit, grapes, but also the result of further activity: in some cases the natural yeast still present in the wort or on the grape skins will work together with the yeast selected and used for the beer, thus changing the flavor profile over time,.

In the world of spontaneous fermentation and beers brewed in barrels, Italy's contribution is also significant, with interesting results that are very topical but not in conflict with tradition. In essence there is no official style, but Italy is making numerous contributions to the world of brewing and putting forward a number of suggestions for making many very contemporary beers.

# CHESTNUT BEER

FAMILY: ALTA E BOTTOM FERMENTATION
CATEGORY: FRUIT BEER
STYLE: CHESTNUT BEER
ORIGIN: ITALY

The use of chestnuts in beer has been one of the hallmarks of the nascent Italian brewing tradition. Chestnuts grow more or less all over Italy: there is hardly a valley, a mountain or a hill where some kind of chestnut does not grow. They are often used as an ingredient in the local cuisine (first or second courses, but also as sweet chestnuts and marrons glacés, and simply as roast chestnuts). The brewers have looked around and found the element of connection with the land, but it is complicated to combine malts, yeasts and chestnuts. It is even hard to find one official style, since every brewer tries to make his different from the rest. The Italian Beer of the Year competition, organized by the Unionbirrai, includes the category "Chestnut beer, top and bottom-fermenting ," recognizing that the chestnut is now well in evidence.

## PRODUCTION

The chestnut is used raw, boiled, minced or in the form of flour, rather than roasted, depending on how the brewer decides to develop the recipe. Some use pure chestnut honey, but then the result should probably be described as honey beer rather than chestnut beer. The choice of malts is free, as is that of hops (not usually a characteristic) and of the type of yeast, which may be top or bottom fermenting.

## CHARACTERISTICS

The appearance is varied, related to the malts selected, as are the bouquet and flavors. In all cases chestnut flavors play a major role, with hints of raw chestnut, roast chestnuts, chestnut or marrons glacés well in evidence and never dominated by the malts, even if they are toasted and roasted, nor by the hops.

Alcohol content: varied.
Pairing: depending on the basic recipe, and also on the possible combinations, any dish that uses chestnuts, from turkey with chestnut stuffing to roasted chestnuts.

# ITALIAN LAGER

FAMILY: BOTTOM FERMENTATION
CATEGORY: PALE LAGER
STYLE: ITALIAN LAGER (style not yet codified and in course of definition)
ORIGIN: ITALY

In fact, Italian lager has not yet developed its own defined, precise style but the growing creativity displayed the numerous small Italian brewers who, not hampered by respect towards a rather unstructured brewing tradition, are moving forward towards the ever more detailed identity of several types of beer that are much appreciated by the local population and further afield.

Among these are Pale Lagers. In Italy as elsewhere, these are still produced on an industrial level by the large national breweries tending towards a rather traditional, bland taste.

Today, on the other hand, a number of independent brewers are making pale, bottom-fermenting beers that are very original and highly sought after. These have a slightly higher alcohol content than other similar styles, with a greater concentration of bitter, resinous and aromatic notes (floral, spicy, fruity) from the hops, that are generously used with dry-hopping, and they often have slightly higher fermentation temperatures than is usual with bottom fermentation to emphasize both olfactory and gustatory sensation.

The annual competition for the best Italian artisanal beers, Beer of the Year 2014, has a special category was reserved for this particular type of beer.

In the international beer panorama, this could be seen as a distortion of the style, but that is how innovation happens. Only history, which has seen so many styles invented, modified and disappear before sometimes being revived again, will know the fate of this Italian trend that is admittedly still in its infancy but full of dynamism and potential.

# DENMARK AND NORWAY

These two countries are treated together not so much because they are both on the North Sea but because they are the perfect example of modernization in brewing.

In the past the Danish brewing scene was literally dominated by Carlsberg. Founded in 1847 by Jacob Christian Jacobsen, one of a family of brewers, Carlsberg became a brewing giant through the insight and investments of its founder and his descendants. Its imprint is evident on the beers drunk in Denmark and throughout the world. Isolated by Emil Christian Hansen, mentioned earlier, *Saccharomyces carlsbergensis* is known today the "founder" of bottom-fermenting yeasts, used in beers all over the world.

Today Denmark is a turmoil of brewing innovation, particularly thanks to Mikkel Borg Bjergs, one of the most famous "gypsy brewers" (a brewer without brewery who therefore produces beer at other breweries) who founded the Mikkeller brand that has shaken Danish tradition (and tranquility).

Mikkeller and other brewers (with or without breweries) such as Amager, Beer Here and Mikkel's twin Jeppe with his Evil Twin (now with its headquarters in Brooklyn, USA) have brought back liveliness to the Danish movement. They have blazed new trails in beer-making with the shameless use of hops from all over the world, particular cereals and the use of maturing in wood. Obviously marketing is very important to establish a foothold, especially for those who do not have their own production plant, and it also helps launch innovative beers, giving them a place of their own on the market.

Further north across the sea, in Norway, after more than 100 years of nothing but

industrial lagers, traditional brewing was revived in 1989 with a brew pub, Oslo Mikrobryggeri, and this paved the way for many other openings. Today Norway is especially inspired by innovations from the United States, so much so that Mike Murphy, a brewer from Philadelphia, after leaving his very individual mark on the Italian and Danish brewing scene, now lives in Stavanger in Norway where he is the master brewer of Lervig Aktiebryggeri.

There are other brewers such as Haandbryggeriet in Drammen and Nøgne Ø in Grimstad that also liven up the local brewing scene. They are helping to get Norwegian brewing innovations known abroad by collaborating with other brewers, participating in events and fairs round the world, many of them small but with great media coverage, as well as exporting a large proportion of their best products. But above all the micro-breweries are shaking up the local market, accustomed to the usual bland production, with their fragrant, aromatic beers. It is worth pointing out that in less than ten years of activity, Nøgne has already produced over 100 different beers while HaandBryggeriet has produced over 70 in much the same time.

Hops does not grow easily along the fjords of the Norwegian coast since the region is too far north, so brewers have to import them from abroad. This partly explains the extensive casual use of hops from North America and Australasia that are then combined with ingredients cultivated locally, such as some cereals (for instance rye) or berries and local fruit for some special beers. But it is with their interpretation of the Anglo-American inspired IPA that the Norwegians really distinguish themselves, in particular those with the addition of rye malt to the cereal grist. Also it has become customary in micro-breweries to use of barrels to mature the beers.

# BALTIC PORTER

FAMILY: BOTTOM FERMENTATION
(but some examples use top fermentation)
CATEGORY: PORTER
STYLE: BALTIC PORTER
ORIGIN: BALTIC SEA COUNTRIES

These are dark beers halfway between Robust Porter and the Russian Imperial Stout. This style has its roots in the 19th century trade of English Porter beers, ales that were extremely popular in the countries round the Baltic Sea and in Russia. These gave rise to today's Baltic Porter that is probably more similar to the Porter of the past, a stronger, structured and intense interpretation of the English Brown Porter of today.

## PRODUCTION

The great difference is that these beers, mainly produced in the region of the Baltic and no longer in England, are brewed using bottom-fermenting yeast, and they are therefore not ales but lagers (although there are a few top-fermenting examples where the temperatures are kept very low).

To ensure that notes of toast and burnt do not dominate, brewers use modern dark malts with the bitterness removed (as is done for Schwarzbier) as well as large amounts of Munich and Vienna malts together with some Crystal.

## CHARACTERISTICS

These have a color between very dark copper and brown, but never black, with a thick, lasting foam, the color of cappuccino. They do not have the strong roast coffee aroma typical of Russian Imperial Stout, but they have intense malty notes similar to those of English Brown Porter as well as fruity esters (raisins, black cherries, blackcurrant) and elegant alcoholic notes.

They are typically sweetish at the start but then balanced by the dark malts that emerge, leading to a mellow finish, enhanced by hints of coffee and liquorice.

The full, generous body is lightened by the high carbonation.

An interesting, complex beer that is nonetheless sufficiently accessible.

Alcohol content: about 5.5-9.5% abv.
Pairing: with roast meat and smoked dishes.

# RYE IPA

FAMILY: TOP FERMENTATION
CATEGORY: NOT YET DEFINED
STYLE: RYE IPA (BUT NOT YET DEFINED)
ORIGIN: UNITED STATES

This style, not yet officially recognized, is based on the IPAs produced with a very unusual ingredient: rye. This rustic cereal, less well-known than barley, is much used throughout the world to produce specialties such as rye bread, rye whisky and the traditional rye beers of Bavaria such as the Roggenbier or the very unusual Finnish Sahti. But it should not be confused with the very new Rye IPA, sometimes known as Rye PA to make it easier to pronounce.

These beers became extremely successful. At first they were only marketed in the United States, after "Hop Rod Rye" produced by the micro-brewery Bear Republic (an example of an Imperial IPA produced with large amounts of rye malt) won several awards in official competitions in the first decade of this century.
Soon avant-garde brewers in Scandinavia also began to experiment very successfully with this type of beer. This is why we decided to include them in the chapter devoted to Denmark and Norway.

In these beers the characteristics of the American IPA have been further enriched by the complex spicy, peppery and earthy profile of rye that adds a certain dryness to the finish.

Alcohol content: about 6-8% abv.

# SMOKED BEERS AND
# BEERS MATURED IN WOOD

According to legend, on one of the occasions that Bamberg Cathedral caught fire, the malt warehouse in the brewery next door became filled with smoke, but the brewer used the malt anyway to make his usual Märzen. When the beer was tasted it was found to taste of smoke, but fortunately the customers loved it. And so the Bamberg Rauchbiers were born. Whether the story is true or not, the smoky beers of Franconia are still around today, as is the cathedral, which was rebuilt. They are beers with characteristics that vary enormously. Most of them vary in color between golden and brown; they are medium bodied with medium-high carbonation and an alcohol content ranging between 4.8 and 6%. The characteristic smoky notes depend on the amount of "rauch" (smoky) malt present in the grist (the proportion ranges between 20 and 100 %). They are accompanied in various degrees by aromas of caramel, toast and even a few herbaceous notes of hops, or on the other hand these may be completely dominant. The only certainty is the yeast: all the beers produced in Franconia are bottom-fermented.

But in fact, wandering around Franconia, you will discover so many beers that stray slightly from these parameters, with lower or higher smoky notes, thin-bodied beers and full-bodied beers. In other words, so much for the Purity Law in this part of Franconia, where every brewer does his own thing, starting with a bottom-fermented beer (Bock, Hefe-Weizen, Dunkel, Schwarz, Doppelbock or Hell), then transforming it into a smoky beer.

Not far from the German border in eastern Prussia, we find the Grodziskie or Grätzer (in Polish or German respectively) beers that are produced exclusively with oak-smoked wheat malt. In the city of Grodzisk (Grätz in German), the last brewery producing this particular type of beer was taken over and closed by another brewer in the Heineken Group. Considered a historic beer and practically extinct, it was recently revived by enthusiasts who through archeological beer research managed to find cells of the original yeast and brought this particular smoked beer back to life in Holland and Germany. It is now possible to find examples of Grätzer beers in the United States. Originally there were only two types, one more alcoholic, which then gave way to a less alcoholic version when a new tax regime came into force.

*Smoked and peaty beers must express smoky aromas in both bouquet and taste but they can be any color: clear, amber or dark.*

In the rest of the world brewers, partly inspired by German tradition and partly driven by their own creativity, are producing smoked beers. These are based on already existing beers, such as Porter, Robust Porter and others, to which smoked malt is added, smoked with whatever wood is found locally and in some cases even with peat. This "macro" category also includes German examples based on Pils beers, on Weizenbock and others, so there are no specifications or limitations regarding alcohol, color, body or gas content. The only constraint concerns the smoking that must be used, the type of smoked malt defining its character in terms of both aroma and flavor.

While there is a very wide range of smoked beers, there is a category that is if possible even wider: beers matured in wooden barrels. Wood, normally used in the past for maturing beers, was gradually replaced by stainless steel, except in a few cases, all of them in Belgium, in Flanders to be precise, where beer is produced by spontaneous fermentation. However many brewers have now started using barrels again to give a character to their beers. Many are from commercial labels that, after more or less time in wood, change (sometimes getting darker because of oxidation). Notes of vanilla, toasted bread, caramel, almonds, cocoa bean or coffee are often found in these beers, but barrels previously used (for port, sherry, red wine, white wine, rum, Scotch whisky, Irish whiskey, Bourbon whiskey and others) can introduce other flavors and also change the tactile profile (body and dryness) of the original beer. Sometimes slightly acid, lactic and acetic notes are also traceable, as well as the work of the other wild yeasts instead of obvious tannic notes. It all depends on the choice of the brewer and his personal taste, but above all on what mother nature (as well as the length of time and the type of wood) decides to donate to the beer. The United States are the biggest maturers of beer in barrels thanks to the size of their cellars and the availability of barrels on the market. Italy is not doing so badly, often taking over the barrels no longer used by wine estates, that are usually close to the brewery and known to the brewer. In fact, many breweries use barrels from all sources, even those used for balsamic acid, vin santo, grappa and various spirits.

*Some beers matured in wooden barrels have a high level of effervescence due to the action of microorganisms such as* Brettanomyces.

# HOMEMADE
# BEER

FAMILY: YOURS
CATEGORY: WHATEVER YOU LIKE!
STYLE: YOUR PREFERENCE
ORIGIN: YOUR HOME

Home-brewing is not only possible but also great fun!

With just a few pieces of simple equipment, some knowledge of the production process and a strong desire to try home-brewing, it is possible to make beer of whatever style you like, just at home with your own hands. As with all things, it is necessary to apply yourself and practice a lot to obtain the best results. But there is no doubt that the pleasure of drinking beer that you have made yourself or sharing it with friends is very satisfying in itself, even if the results are less than perfect.

It is possible to start with just the fermentation of simple preparations of already-hopped malt extract. These preparations are simply the "concentration" of the work of other brewers who have prepared a normal wort of barley malt, already made bitter with hops. All water has been removed from by boiling it for a long time so that it evaporates. All the novice home-brewer has to do is to add water, dissolve the contents of the container and then make it ferment by inoculating it with a specially prepared yeast. Then, as already mentioned, it will the yeast that does the rest and makes the beer.

On the other hand, for those who do not like to use concentrates, there is the all-grain production method, that is, starting with grains of cereal that must be milled, mashed, filtered, boiled, hopped and finally… fermented! This procedure, identical to the traditional methods used by brewers, requires more time and effort as well as more space; but in this way you will be able to choose and control every detail of the process when you make beer.

Today there many websites in all countries that sell products for home-brewing, and they often supply professional micro-breweries as well. From these you will be able to obtain high quality raw materials, basic or more advanced equipment, manuals and books on home-brewing techniques, in other words everything you may need and more.

There are also several national associations and movements of home-brewers and enthusiasts who organize meetings, seminars and guided tastings offering training programs, and for the more competitive, they also organize important competitions where home-brewers can put their own creations to the test.

But do not think, as many do, that the step between knowing how to make your own beer at home and setting up as a professional brewer is just a small one: everyone knows how to cook but not everyone is a great chef!

# 24 RECIPES

BY CHEF GIOVANNI RUGGIERI

# PAIRING
# BEER AND FOOD

To accompany a dish with a particular beer, it is necessary to know both elements well. It is important to remember that the objective is to achieve a harmonious balance of taste in the mouth that may be as a result of a contrast (such as sweetness contrasting with bitterness) or of a similarity (bitterness accompanying bitterness or sweetness accompanying sweetness).

An important thing to remember is that the difference between the two elements should not be too great.

For example, it is not a good idea serve a very bitter beer with a very sweet dish: "the distance" between the two elements is hard to bridge in a balanced way.

But equally it is not advisable to serve a very sweet beer with a very sweet dish because that would be excessively sickly. A sweet beer may be a perfect accompaniment for a sweet dish up to a certain point and, when perfectly balanced, it will even reduce the final sensation of sweetness.

The golden rule is that a dish with a delicate flavor will be best with a simple beer while strong and pronounced flavors will benefit from more complex, extreme beers.

In addition to the more basic components of sweetness and bitterness, it is important to remember that there other characteristics of beer to be taken into account, such as the alcoholic strength, the degree of sparkling, the amount of toasting, its acidity, its astringency and its aromatic properties.

Rather than presenting the theory, here are a few simple but important rules that can help and encourage you to experiment without worrying too much: remember that practice is undoubtedly the best way to learn, and that the biggest discoveries are made by accident! You can be relaxed because the wrong combination of food and beer is not a health hazard and it will not ruin a good beer or a good dish: if after the first sip and bite you decide that they do not combine well, you can always enjoy them separately!

# THE COMMONEST PAIRINGS

THE BITTERNESS OF THE HOP BALANCES THE RICHNESS OF FOOD (BY HELPING TO CLEANSE THE MOUTH) AND OF SWEET DISHES; IT EMPHASIZES PIQUANCY AND SPICINESS IN GENERAL; IT GOES WELL WITH BITTER FOODS.

THE SWEETNESS OF THE BEER CONTRASTS WITH THE BITTERNESS, ACIDITY AND SPICINESS OF FOOD.

ACIDITY BALANCES THE RICHNESS AND FATTINESS OF DISHES.

THE TOASTED MALT BALANCES SMOKINESS AND CONTRASTS WITH SWEETNESS.

ALCOHOL CONTRASTS WITH FATS AND ENHANCES SPICINESS.

# SASHIMI OF PIEDMONTESE FASSONA BEEF WITH TURNIP SPROUTS AND PORTER BEER CREAM

SERVES 4

11 1/2 OZ (330 G) PIECES FASSONA BEEF, TRIMMED
1 1/4 CUPS (300 ML) PORTER BEER
1/3 OZ (8 G) LEAF GELATIN
1 SACHET SPARKLE DUSTING POWDER
1 SMALL BOWL TURNIP SPROUTS
EXTRA-VIRGIN OLIVE OIL
SALT
WHITE WINE VINEGAR

PREPARATION

For the cream, put the leaf gelatin in cold water with a few ice cubes for 10 minutes. Pour it into a pan and warm over a low heat for 1 minute while stirring with a whisk until it is completely dissolved. Pour a little beer into the dissolved gelatin while it is still on a very low heat, then add the rest of the beer and put in the refrigerator for 12 hours. The following day, mix in a kitchen mixer until it is creamy and foamy. Leave it to rest in the refrigerator.

To prepare the meat, remove any fat. Cut into slices 1/8 in (3 mm) thick, arrange them in a steel dish and season with a little oil and salt.

For the sprouts, cut off the end parts with scissors and put in a bath of cold water for a few minutes, then drain and season with oil, salt and white wine vinegar to taste.

Plate up, starting with the cream on the bottom of the dish. With the fingers, sprinkle with the sparkle dusting powder, add the slices of fassona beef and finally the turnip sprouts very lightly seasoned, so as not to lose their pungency.

PAIRING BEER AND FOOD

# FRIED COD IN BATTER
# WITH BITTER ALE VINAIGRETTE
# AND WILD LEAF SALAD

SERVES 4

14 OZ (400 G) FRESH COD (GABILO)
1 CUP (150 G) RICE FLOUR
SCANT 1/2 CUP (50 G) TYPE 0 OR ALL-PURPOSE FLOUR
2 CUPS (500 ML) SPARKLING WATER, REFRIGERATED
1/3 CUP+2 TBSP (100 ML) BITTER ALE
3/4 CUP+2 TBSP (200 ML) EXTRA-VIRGIN OLIVE OIL
1/2 OZ (15 G) BREWER'S YEAST
9 OZ (250 G) WILD LEAF SALAD (SMALL RED AND GREEN LEAVES)
PEANUT OIL AS NEEDED
SALT AND PEPPER

PREPARATION

For the vinaigrette, mix the olive oil with the Bitter Ale and salt. Mix with a hand blender until it has emulsified.

For the cod, remove the central spine and cut the fish into pieces about 2 1/2 in (6 cm) square.

For the batter, mix the rice flour and the plain flour. Mix the yeast in a small amount of the water.

Add the rest of the sparkling water, very cold from the refrigerator and just opened. Work the mixture by hand until it forms a thick, creamy mixture. Test it by dipping a piece of cod into it, making sure that it does not drip off immediately. Fry until the batter is crisp but be careful not to let it get brown—it must remain white.

Plate up, putting the wild leaf salad mixed with the vinaigrette on the bottom of the plate and then the pieces of cod just fried in batter.

# PORK FILLET COOKED IN BAVARIAN WEIZEN BEER, BARLEY, CABBAGE AND CUMIN

SERVES 4

1 PORK FILLET
1 1/4 CUPS (300 ML) BAVARIAN WEIZEN BEER
1 TSP (3 G) CUMIN
11 1/2 OZ (330 G) CABBAGE
3 1/2 OZ (100 G) BARLEY
EXTRA-VIRGIN OLIVE OIL
WHITE WINE VINEGAR
SALT AND PEPPER

PREPARATION

For the ham, heat the beer in a pan to 150 °F (65 °C). Meanwhile, remove any fat parts from the pork fillet, season with salt and pepper and rub it with oil, massaging it well so that it is absorbed. Fry the pork fillet in a very hot non-stick pan. Immerse the meat in the hot beer and cook at a constant temperature for 50 minutes. Remove the fillet from the beer, put it on a dish and leave it cool in the refrigerator.

For the barley, boil the salted water and cook the barley in it for the time indicated on the packet. Form the boiled barley into little discs about 3/4 in (2 cm) thick, using a cookie cutter. Season with salt and unfiltered extra-virgin olive oil.

Cut the cabbage into very fine strips, season with extra-virgin olive oil, white wine vinegar, salt and cumin ground in a coffee grinder. Put little heaps of the sliced, seasoned cabbage on the plates. Cut the ham into thin slices and arrange it on the cabbage with the barley to form petals.

# AMBERJACK FILLET COOKED IN BELGIAN ALE WITH YOUNG STEAMED VEGETABLES

SERVES 4

1 AMBERJACK OF 1 1/2 LB (700 G)
2 CUPS (500 ML) BELGIAN ALE
4 NEW ZUCCHINI
4 NEW CARROTS
1 BUNCH FRESH HOPS
EXTRA-VIRGIN OLIVE OIL
SALT AND PEPPER

**PREPARATION**

Fillet the amberjack, removing the little bones with tweezers. Remove the skin with a flexible knife and cut the fillets to make 4 servings.
Bring the beer to the boil, turn off the heat and leave for 5 minutes. Then put the fillets in the beer and leave for 8 minutes. Drain carefully, so that they do not break.

Meanwhile, clean and wash the vegetables. Using a mandolin, cut into slices 1/10 in (2 mm) thick. Cook the vegetables in a steamer for 4 minutes and season with oil, salt and pepper.

Arrange the vegetables on plates, alternating them by color, and add the fish fillets. Serve at room temperature.

# TUNA-RABBIT
# WITH SEASONAL VEGETABLES
# AND GELATIN WITH PILS

SERVES 4

4 RABBIT LEGS
1 ZUCCHINI
1 FENNEL BULB
1/2 RED AND 1/2 YELLOW BELL PEPPER
2 STALKS CELERY
1 CARROT
2 WHITE ONIONS
4 PODS FLAT BEANS
1 BUNCH FRESH TARRAGON
8 LEAVES GELATIN
4 CUPS (1 LITER) PILS
1 BUNCH FRESH CURLY-LEAVED PARSLEY
EXTRA-VIRGIN OLIVE OIL
RED WINE VINEGAR
SALT AND PEPPER

**PREPARATION**

Brown the rabbit legs having seasoned them with salt and pepper. Dice the carrot, one stick of celery and one onion. Brown them in a high-sided baking dish. Add the rabbit legs to the vegetable mixture, mix in half the butter and bake covered at 300 °F (150 °C) for about one and a half hours.

Meanwhile clean, wash and cut the remaining vegetables into lozenges 3/4 to 1 1/4 in (2 to 3 cm) long. Cook the vegetables separately, browning them in a little extra-virgin olive oil over a high heat, then immediately afterwards add a little water and continue until it has almost completely evaporated. Once the cooking is finished, remove the rabbit legs from the pan, wait for a few minutes and then remove the meat from the bone, shredding it. Combine the vegetables with the rabbit meat and strain the cooking water into a pan. Add the remaining beer and the leaves of gelatin previously softened in cold water, then stir until it is completely dissolved. Pour the liquid into the dish with the shredded meat and vegetables. Cover with food grade plastic wrap in contact with the meat and the vegetables so that the surface of the mixture is even. Leave to rest in the refrigerator for at least one hour. Chop the tarragon and parsley separately. Season and finish the gelatin with extra-virgin olive oil, salt, pepper, parsley, tarragon and a little red wine vinegar. Serve at room temperature.

# COTECHINO SAUSAGE COOKED IN SMOKED BEER WITH SEASONAL VEGETABLES IN SWEET AND SOUR SAUCE

SERVES 4

5 1/4 OZ (150 G) NEW WHITE ONIONS
5 1/4 OZ (150 G) FENNEL
5 1/4 OZ (150 G) RED BELL PEPPERS
5 1/4 OZ (150 G) YELLOW BELL PEPPERS
5 1/4 OZ (150 G) CAULIFLOWER
5 1/4 OZ (150 G) CARROTS
2 CUPS (400 G) SUGAR
4 CUPS (1 LITER) WHITE WINE VINEGAR
2 TBSP (40 G) SALT
12 OZ (380 G) COTECHINO SAUSAGES
4 CUPS (1 LITER) SMOKED BEER

PREPARATION

Bring the beer with 8 cups (2 liters) of water to the boil. Immerse the cotechino sausages and cook for one and a half hours.

Meanwhile, clean the vegetables, wash them and cut into cubes. Then cook in the vinegar with the sugar and salt, reducing until the vinegar has the consistency of a sleek syrup, but not as thick as honey. When the sausages are cooked, cut them into pieces 1 1/4 in (3 cm) thick and remove the skin.

Serve, placing the pieces of sausage on the vegetables.

# TRIPEL ALE RISOTTO

SERVES 4

14 OZ (400 G) VIALONE NANO RICE
7 OZ (200 G) PARMIGIANO REGGIANO
6 TBSP (90 G) BUTTER
8 CUPS (2 LITERS) TRIPEL ALE
1 BUNCH RADISH SHOOTS
EXTRA-VIRGIN OLIVE OIL
SALT AND PEPPER

PREPARATION

Boil the ale in a pan and remove 3/4 cup+2 tbsp (200 ml) from it.
Cook the vialone nano rice in extra-virgin olive oil and salt. When the grains are very hot to the touch, start to cook the rice with the Tripel ale and cook for 12 minutes, stirring the rice.
When cooked, add the butter, the Parmigiano Reggiano, a few grinds of pepper and the ale previously removed. Cook the rice, stirring it until it is creamy and soft.

Wash the radish shoots in cold water, cutting them off the radishes with a small pair of scissors.

Serve the risotto in the plates, decorating with a few radish shoots.

# STOUT SPAGHETTI
# WITH A REDUCTION OF SHRIMPS

SERVES 4

3 CUPS (500 G) DURUM WHEAT SEMOLINA FLOUR
3/4 CUP (180 ML) STOUT
1 TSP (4 ML) COGNAC
3 LB 5 OZ (1.5 KG) RAW SHRIMPS
1 ONION
2 TBSP (20 G) TOMATO PASTE
3/4 CUP+5 TBSP (200 ML) WHITE WINE
1 STICK CELERY
1 CLOVE GARLIC
1 BUNCH FRESH OREGANO

PREPARATION

For the pasta, mix the flour and beer in a bowl to make a moist, uneven mixture. Put the mixture through a fresh pasta machine and make spaghetti, cut to a length of 6 in (15 cm). If a pasta machine is not available, use ready-made spaghetti and cook it in water and beer (4 cups/1 liter beer and the rest water).

Clean the shrimps, removing the shell and the head. Put the remains in a pan with a little oil, the onion, clove of garlic unpeeled, the celery, the tomato paste and the cognac. Cover with the cold water and simmer on a very low heat until the liquid is reduced by two-thirds. Strain the sauce into a pan through a very fine sieve.

Cook the spaghetti, cut the shrimps into pieces and, once the pasta is cooked, stir in the reduction, the raw shrimps and the extra-virgin olive oil. Serve, finishing the dish with some leaves of fresh oregano.

# LITTLE RED POTATO GNOCCHI WITH BARLEY MALT IN FISH STOCK WITH SHOOTS

SERVES 4

4 LB 6 OZ (2 KG) RED POTATOES
3 EGG YOLKS
2 1/2 OZ (70 G) BARLEY MALT
3 TSP (20 G) SALT
2 1/2 OZ (70 G) PARMIGIANO REGGIANO, GRATED
2 1/2 CUPS (300 G) PLAIN TYPE 0 OR ALL-PURPOSE FLOUR
2 LB 3 OZ (1 KG) CLAMS
2 LB 3 OZ (1 KG) MUSSELS
1 LB 2 OZ (500 G) COCKLES
1 SEA BREAM, ABOUT 11 1/2 OZ (330 G)
1 BUNCH PARSLEY
1 BOWL MIXED SPROUTS
3/4 CUP+5 TBSP WHITE WINE
3 1/2 OZ (100 G) TOMATO PASSATA
EXTRA-VIRGIN OLIVE OIL
SALT AND PEPPER

**PREPARATION**

Boil the potatoes in their skins. Meanwhile prepare the egg yolks, salt, Parmigiano Reggiano, barley malt and flour, keeping them separate. Once the potatoes have cooked, peel them quickly while they are still very hot, mash them with a potato masher on a work surface and leave to cool. To the potatoes, add the egg yolks, malt, salt, Parmigiano Reggiano and finally the flour. Knead the mixture quickly, so that it does not become wet, cut into pieces, roll them on the surface to form long cylinders, then cut into pieces about 3/4 in (2 cm) long and roll into dumplings. Place the dumplings on a tray covered with baking parchment and put in the freezer, making sure they do not stick to each other.

For the broth, clean the sea bream. Soak clams and cockles in salted water, remove the beards from the mussels. Fry all the molluscs in extra-virgin olive oil for 3 minutes with the parsley stalks, pour on the white wine, add the tomatoes and the whole sea bream, cover with cold water and bring to a very gentle boil. Let it reduce by half and then filter it through a fine mesh strainer. Cook the gnocchi in salted water in another pot, drain and serve directly on the plates, cover with fish stock prepared earlier, a dash of raw extra-virgin olive oil, and finally the washed shoots.

# TAGLIATELLE WITH RABBIT RAGU
# IN AMERICAN PALE ALE
# AND SAUTEED HOPS

SERVES 4

4 CUPS (500 G) PLAIN TYPE 0 OR ALL-PURPOSE FLOUR
15 EGG YOLKS
1 STICK CELERY
1 CARROT
1 WHITE ONION
4 TBSP (40 G) TOMATO PASTE
1 LB 2 OZ (500 G) RABBIT MEAT, CHOPPED
2 CUPS (500 G) AMERICAN PALE ALE
1 BUNCH FRESH HOPS
EXTRA-VIRGIN OLIVE OIL
SALT AND PEPPER

PREPARATION

For the pasta, pour the flour on a pastry board, add the egg yolks and knead until the mixture is compact, smooth and elastic. Cut the pasta into sheets and roll them out one by one with a rolling pin to make sheets about 1/25 in (1 mm) thick. Roll out the sheets and cut into strips no wider than 3/16 in (5 mm). Form skeins with the tagliatelle just made and arrange them in bowl sprinkled with flour, then put in the refrigerator.

Wash and clean the hops, dry them and put them in the refrigerator.
Chop the onion, celery and carrot, sweat in a pan with a little oil, add the meat and continue browning.
Then add the beer, the tomato puree, salt and pepper and cook for 1 hour.
Bring a pan of salted water to the boil, cook the tagliatelle for 3 minutes and dress with the sauce.

Before serving, sauté the hops on a high heat for 2 minutes in a pan with a little extra-virgin olive oil and salt, then add to the finished dish.

PAIRING BEER AND FOOD

# ROUGHLY CUT PASTA WITH BARLEY MALT, WHIPPED CHEESE AND BALTIC PORTER

SERVES 4

4 CUPS (500 G) PLAIN TYPE 0 OR ALL-PURPOSE FLOUR
3 1/2 OZ (100 G) BARLEY MALT IN SYRUP
3 EGGS
7 OZ (200 G) CHEESE
1 1/3 CUPS (330 ML) BALTIC PORTER
SCANT 1/4 CUP (50 G) BUTTER
SALT AND PEPPER

### PREPARATION

For the pasta, turn the flour onto a pastry board, then add the eggs and the malt. Knead until the mixture is smooth, even and compact. Cut the pasta into sheets and roll the pasta with a narrow rolling pin to a thickness of 1/25 in (1 mm). Cut the sheets into irregular pieces, as the name of the pasta suggests.

Heat the butter in a casserole and add the beer, raising the heat to the maximum. With a rotary movement of the arm, mix the melted butter and the beer so that it forms a reduction. Put a pan of salted water on the heat and bring it to the boil. Then cook the pasta for 4 minutes, drain, then mix with the beer and butter emulsion. Plate it up, sprinkling it with cheese grated earlier.

# RAVIOLI ALLA FONDUTA AND DUBBEL JELLY WITH BUTTER AND SAGE

SERVES 4

2 1/2 CUPS (300 G) PLAIN FLOUR TYPE 2
1 CUP (200 G) DURUM WHEAT SEMOLINA FLOUR
18 EGG YOLKS
10 1/2 OZ (300 G) FONTINA
1 1/4 CUPS (300 ML) MILK
1 TSP (5 G) AGAR AGAR
2 CUPS (500 ML) DUBBEL BEER
SCANT 1/2 CUP (100 G) BUTTER
SAGE
SALT AND PEPPER

**PREPARATION**

Infuse the fontina cheese cut into dice in a bowl of milk for at least 2 hours, after which dissolve the cheese in a bain marie, stirring the mixture. Whisk with an immersion blender to make it smooth and even. Put it in a plastic bag and leave to cool. Once it is cool it must be compact.

Put the beer in a casserole, add the agar agar, mix it with whisk while cold, put the casserole on the heat and continue to mix until the beer has come to the boil. Then remove it immediately from the heat. Cool it well in the refrigerator, then whisk the gelatin with the immersion blender so as to make a homogenous cream with the same consistency as jam. Put the mixture in a plastic bag and put it in the refrigerator.

For the pasta, mix the two flours and arrange on a pastry board in a mound. Add the egg yolks and mix until it is compact, elastic and smooth. Cut the pasta into sheets and roll it out with a fine rolling pin until it is 1/25 in (1 mm) thick. Then arrange little knobs of beer gelatin and cheese on the sheet. Cover with another sheet of pasta and seal the two layers together, by moistening them. Cut the pasta with a pastry wheel to make ravioli. Cook for 4 minutes in salted water, then stir into the butter already salted and melted in the bowl in which you have browned the sage.

Serve very hot on a flat dish.

# GRIDDLED SQUID WITH A REDUCTION OF HELL AND SUGAR-SNAP PEAS WITH BEER VINAIGRETTE

### SERVES 4

4 SQUID, ABOUT 7 OZ (200 G) EACH
14 OZ (400 G) SUGAR-SNAP PEAS
1/3 CUP (100 ML) HELL BEER
1/3 CUP (100 ML) EXTRA-VIRGIN OLIVE OIL
4 TSP (20 ML) RED WINE VINEGAR
3 TSP (7 G) TAPIOCA FLOUR
SALT AND PEPPER

### PREPARATION

Put the beer in a pan with the tapioca flour. Bring to the boil on a gentle heat and stir continually with a whisk until the mixture thickens. Cool in the refrigerator. Using an immersion blender, emulsify the oil, the cooled beer mixture, salt, pepper and vinegar to make a vinaigrette. Add the sugar-snap peas blanched in salted water for 4 minutes.

Cut the squid in half. Remove the skin and entrails. Cut slits in the flesh with a knife, making a grid of lines at right angles to each other, while being careful not to cut through the flesh entirely. This process makes the squid soft and crisp at the same time. Wash and dry the squid, then add salt and season the squid with oil. Cook on a hot griddle for 5 to 7 minutes.

Serve the squid with the sugar-snap peas, decorating the dish with a few drops of the vinaigrette.

# ROAST POUSSIN WITH INDIA PALE ALE AND POTATOES STUFFED WITH PIQUANT SAUCE

SERVES 4

4 POUSSINS, 1 LB 2 OZ (500 G) EACH
2 CUPS (500 ML) INDIA PALE ALE
1 LB 5 OZ (600 G) POTATOES
3 1/2 OZ (100 G) FRESH TOMATOES
1 OZ (30 G) SPICY RED CHILI PEPPER, FRESH
1 BUNCH CHERVIL
3 EGGS
ROSEMARY
EXTRA-VIRGIN OLIVE OIL
BAY LEAF
THYME
SALT AND PEPPER

PREPARATION

Season the poussins with salt and pepper, then immerse them in the beer with the aromatic herbs. Let them marinate for at least 10 minutes. Drain the poussins and dry them, then saute in a little oil in a non-stick pan. Transfer the pan into the oven preheated to 375 °F (190 °C), basting them with the beer marinade previously brought to the boil. Cook for 35 minutes.

In the meantime, wash and clean the peppers, cut into pieces and beat with olive oil and salt until creamy. Brown in a pan for 4 minutes, then add the tomatoes, washed and cut into pieces, and season with salt. Cook until the sauce is reduced.

Boil the potatoes in their skins in salted water. When cooked, peel them quickly and mash them in a bowl with a potato masher. Then add the egg yolks and mix, seasoning the mixture. Add the whites whipped to snow, gently folding them in, and pour the mixture onto a baking sheet lined with a sheet of parchment paper. With your hands lightly greased with oil, spread out the mixture to a thickness of 3/16 in (5 mm). Cook in the oven at 350 °F (180 °C) for 15 minutes.

Take out the soft potato biscuit and cut into 3-inch (8-centimeter) squares. Spread them with the spicy sauce and form into lasagnette (wide ribbon noodles), overlapping them. Garnish wih rosemary leaves. Serve the poussins with the potatoes, garnishing with thyme leaves.

# GLAZED PORK KNUCKLE
# WITH SMALL RED FRUITS, RASPBERRY BEER
# DROPS AND CREAMED POTATO

SERVES 4

2 PORK KNUCKLES CUT IN HALF LENGTHWAYS
1 STICK CELERY
1 CARROT
1 WHITE ONION
1 1/4 CUPS (300 ML) WHITE WINE
1 BUNCH HERBS CONSISTING OF BAY LEAF, ROSEMARY, THYME, SAGE
1 BOWL RASPBERRIES
1 BOWL BLACKBERRIES
1 BOWL BLUEBERRIES
3/4 CUP+2 TBSP (200 ML) FRAMBOISE BEER
2 TSP (5 G) TAPIOCA FLOUR
2 LB 2 OZ (1 KG) YELLOW POTATOES
1 1/4 CUPS (300 ML) FRESH CREAM
3 TBSP (40 G) BUTTER
EXTRA-VIRGIN OLIVE OIL
SALT AND PEPPER

PREPARATION

Peel and wash the celery, carrot and onion, cut into cubes and fry in an ovenproof pan with olive oil and salt. Salt and pepper the pork knuckles, saute in a non-stick pan, pour in the white wine, add the red fruits having previously washed them and bring to a boil. Pour the sauce over the knuckles in the pan, add the bouquet garni, and cook in the oven for 2 hours at 350 °F (180 °C).

Put the beer in a saucepan, add the tapioca flour and bring to the boil, stirring quickly with a whisk until it forms a thick sauce. Leave to cool.

Boil the potatoes in their skins in salted water. Drain and peel them, crush them in a pan, add the very cold butter, stir until it is well blended, add salt, add the cold cream and transfer to the heat, stirring until you have a puree. Remove the knuckles from the oven, transfer to a serving dish, and then reduce the strained sauce until it is thick and glossy.

Cover the knuckles with the sauce, add the mashed potatoes to the dish and garnish with a few drops of the beer and tapioca sauce.

# FILET OF RED MULLET WITH MASHED POTATOES AND BIÈRE BLANCHE WITH SPROUTS AND YOUNG LEAVES

SERVES 4

12 RED MULLET, ABOUT 3 1/2 OZ (100 G)
1 LB 2 OZ (500 G) YELLOW POTAIOESE
1 1/4 CUPS (300 ML) BIÈRE BLANCHE
1 BUNCH ARUGULA
1 BUNCH VALERIAN
1 BUNCH LOOSE-LEAF CURLY LETTUCE
1 BUNCH CASTELFRANCO RADICCHIO
1 BUNCH MIXED WILD LEAF SALAD
1 BUNCH ENDIVE
3/4 CUP+2 TBSP (200 ML) WHITE WINE
EXTRA-VIRGIN OLIVE OIL
SALT AND PEPPER

**PREPARATION**

Boil the potatoes in salted boiling water for 45 minutes.

Wash all the salad leaves in cold water, drain the excess water, place them in a container and put in the refrigerator. Fillet and bone the mullet. Keep them in the refrigerator until ready to use, covered with a moistened paper towel.

Once the potatoes are cooked, drain and peel them and put them in a blender, add the beer, salt, add extra virgin olive oil and blend until creamy. Heat a non-stick pan greased with olive oil, and saute the red mullet fillets already salted, and also part of the skin. After 2 minutes of browning, pour in the white wine. Let the wine reduce until it becomes creamy.

Pour the potato cream into a shallow dish forming a layer 3/8 in (1 cm) thick. Add the salad greens dressed with extra virgin olive oil and salt, and finally the red mullet fillets with the sauce in which they were cooked.

# LAMB IN A HERB CRUST WITH A LAGER REDUCTION AND CREAM OF CHARD

SERVES 4

2 RACKS OF LAMB
1 BUNCH PARSLEY, THYME, ROSEMARY
SCANT 1/2 CUP (100 G) BUTTER
3 1/2 OZ (100 G) BREADCRUMBS
3/4 CUP+2 TBSP (200 ML) LAGER BEER
2 TSP (5 G) TAPIOCA FLOUR
14 OZ (400 G) FRESH BEETS
2 TSP (4 G) AGAR AGAR
EXTRA-VIRGIN OLIVE OIL
SALT AND PEPPER

### PREPARATION

Blend the bread crumbs with the butter, herb leaves and a little salt to make a thick and slightly grainy mixture. Compact it with your hands and place it on a sheet of parchment paper. Put another sheet of parchment paper on top and roll out with a rolling pin until the herb crust is 1/8 in (3 mm) thick. Put in the refrigerator to harden.

Brown the racks of lamb previously salted and peppered in a non-stick pan and let them rest on a baking sheet. Stick the layers of herb crust to the racks of lamb and bake for 12 minutes at 375 °F (190 °C).
Wash the beets, blanch them in salted water for 2 minutes, then drain and leave to cool in iced water. Squeeze them, sprinkle with agar agar and put in a saucepan after passing the mixture through a medium-meshed sieve. Bring to the boil, stirring with a whisk, then leave it cool in the refrigerator to make a firm jelly. Then whisk with an immersion blender until it reaches the consistency of a very smooth cream, and season with salt.

Put the beer and tapioca flour in a saucepan, bring to a boil, stirring with a whisk to a thick cream.
Cut the rack of lamb in half, put the cream of beets on the plates, add a few drops of reduction of beer and finally lay the lamb on top.

# PANCETTA COOKED IN KÖLSCH WITH SAVOY CABBAGE SALAD AND A BARLEY MALT REDUCTION

SERVES 4

14 OZ (400 G) FRESH PANCETTA
1 SAVOY CABBAGE
2 OZ (50 G) BARLEY GRAINS
2 OZ (50 G) BARLEY MALT IN SYRUP
4 CUPS (1 LITER) KÖLSCH BEER
EXTRA-VIRGIN OLIVE OIL
WHITE WINE VINEGAR
SALT AND PEPPER

**PREPARATION**

Cut the bacon into 4 pieces forming 4 cubes, add salt and pepper and brown in a hot non-stick pan. Seal the meat on all sides and dip it in beer previously boiled in a saucepan. Cook over very low heat for 1 hour.

In the meantime boil the barley grain for 10 minutes in 1 1/4 cups (300 ml) of salt water, add to the cooking water, in which you have drained the barley and the malted barley, stir well and strain into another saucepan. Reduce on the stove until the mixture is thick. Remove the bacon from the beer and let it brown in the oven with the grill on for 5 minutes, until the fat of the meat begins to sizzle, but without letting it take color.

Cut the cabbage into thin strips, wash and drain. Toss with extra-virgin olive oil, salt, pepper and white vinegar. Coat the bacon with the reduction of barley malt and place it on the cabbage salad.

# HOT CHOCOLATE PIE WITH IMPERIAL RUSSIAN STOUT AND A COATING OF 72% FINE CHOCOLATE

### SERVES 4

3 1/2 OZ (100 G) BITTER CHOCOLATE POWDER
1 CUP (230 G) BUTTER
1 1/2 CUPS (300 G) SUGAR
4 EGGS
1 1/2 CUPS (200 G) PLAIN TYPE 0 OR ALL-PURPOSE FLOUR
1 1/4 CUPS (300 ML) IMPERIAL RUSSIAN STOUT (PEATY IF POSSIBLE)

FOR THE COVERING
12 OZ (350 G) 72% FONDANT CHOCOLATE AT ROOM TEMPERATURE

**PREPARATION**

For the cake, cream the butter with the sugar in a mixer with a whisk until well blended (at least 15 minutes). When the butter is creamy white and has incorporated the air, add one egg at a time and beat until the egg is fully incorporated, continuing until all the eggs are mixed in. Then reduce the speed of the beater and add the sifted cocoa powder previously passed through a fine mesh sieve, then the flour also finely sieved. Finally when the flour is well mixed in, pour in the beer in a stream.

Grease some aluminum molds with butter and then sugar them inside. Put each one on an electronic kitchen scale and add 3 oz (80 g) of the dough to each mold. Put them on a tray and, one by one, gently tap the bottom of each glass so as to eliminate any air in the dough. Then put them in the refrigerator

Cook the cakes in a preheated oven at 375 °F (190 °C) for 12 minutes. Remove from the oven and after waiting 2 minutes turn the cakes out of the molds. Put each one in the center of the plate.

For the coating, take a pasta machine, set the rollers to a thickness of 1/12 in (2 mm) and pass the chocolate mixture through it, making delicate sheets. Cover each cake with a sheet. It is advisable to move quickly so that the coating sheets do not melt too much once they are resting on the hot cakes.

# SOFT HAZELNUT COOKIES WITH BROWN ALE FOAM AND CRESS

### SERVES 4

**FOR THE COOKIES**
2 EGGS
1 CUP (200 G) SUGAR
7 OZ (200 G) HAZELNUT PASTE
1 1/4 CUPS (160 G) FLOUR

**FOR THE FOAM**
2 CUPS (500 ML) BROWN ALE
1/3 OZ (8 G) LEAF GELATIN
1 CUP (100 G) CANE SUGAR
1 BUNCH FRESH CRESS

### PREPARATION

For the cookies, whisk the eggs and sugar with an electric mixer until the mixture is fluffy and light in color. Add the hazelnut paste and stir gently so as not to diminish the mass. Finally, add the sifted flour and mix well together. Line a medium-sized roasting pan with parchment paper, butter it and pour in the mixture, spreading it to a thickness of 1 in (25 mm). Bake in a preheated oven at 350 °F (180 °C) for 12 minutes. Take out of the the oven, remove from the pan and cut into rectangles, then leave to cool at room temperature

For the foam, melt 1/3 cup (100 ml) of beer and the cane sugar in a pan on the heat, add the leaves of gelatin previously soaked in cold water, and stir to dissolve completely. Add the remaining beer and pour into a syphon with 2 charges of nitrogen, shake well for at least 3 minutes and store in refrigerator.

Clean the watercress, wash and dry. Serve the cake by placing a cookie in the center of each plate. Spray the beer foam on the cookies and then add the cress sprouts, which will give a spicy note to the dish.

# RASPBERRY SOUP, GOSE BEER GRANITA AND CARAMEL SAUCE

### SERVES 4

#### FOR THE SOUP
1/3 CUP (100 ML) ACACIA HONEY
GRATED LEMON ZEST
6 CUPS FRESH RASPBERRIES

#### FOR THE BEER DROPS
3/4 CUP+2 TBSP (200 ML) GOSE BEER
1/2 CUP (100 G) SUGAR

#### FOR THE CARAMEL SAUCE
1 OZ (30 G) BARLEY MALT
1 1/2 CUPS (300 G) SUGAR
1 CUP (150 ML) WATER

### PREPARATION

For the soup, wash the raspberries and very carefully dry them with absorbent paper towels. Put them in a jug, add the honey and lemon zest, then blend with the immersion blender. Strain the mixture through a chinois with small holes into another container to remove all the seeds and put in the refrigerator.

For the beer drops, boil the beer with the sugar and reduce by two-thirds on a low heat. Turn the mixture into a baking dish, put it in the freezer and every 20 minutes (5 times in all), mix it with fork, so that when it begins to solidify it takes on the consistency of a granita.

For the caramel sauce, put a generous 2/3 cup (100 milliliters) water, the sugar and the malt in a bowl and mix. Bring to the boil until the sugar starts to brown, then remove from the hear, let it rest for few seconds, then add the rest of the water. Carefully mix and put in the refrigerator for a few minutes.

At the time of serving, divide the soup between 4 deep bowls, add the granita and let a few drops of caramel fall on the dish from a spoon.

# AMERICAN LAGER AND MINT JELLY WITH STRAWBERRY AND GINGER SALSA

### SERVES 4

#### FOR THE JELLY
2 1/2 CUPS (600 ML) AMERICAN LAGER
1 1/2 CUPS (300 G) CANE SUGAR
15 LEAVES GELATIN
5 1/4 OZ (150 G) FRESH MINT LEAVES

#### FOR THE SALSA
7 OZ (200 G) STRAWBERRIES
2/3 OZ (20 G) FRESH GINGER
1/2 CUP (100 G) SUGAR
LEMON ZEST

### PREPARATION

For the jelly, put the leaves of gelatin in cold water with a little ice for 10 minutes. Heat half the beer in a pan with the cane sugar and bring to the boil. Turn off the heat, add the squeezed leaves of gelatin and melt, then add the mint leaves and leave to infuse for 20 minutes at room temperature. Add the remaining beer and mix.

Take some small metal cups and arrange them on a baking sheet covered with ice and a little water. Pour the mixture into each cup to a level of 3/4 inch (2 centimeters) and add a mint leaf vertically. Keep he mint leaf vertical until the gelatin has set, then add a little mint just chopped into julienne strips. Add 3/4 in (2 cm) more of the mixture and again hold the mint leaf vertical, so that it is not completely immersed in the gelatin. Put the little cups in the refrigerator and leave to cool for at least 2 hours. If you can, prepare the jelly the previous day, so that it will have the right consistency.

For the strawberry and ginger salsa, beat the strawberries together with the sugar, the ginger and the lime zest. Pass it through a fine sieve to remove the seeds.

Serve by placing a disc of salsa in the center of the plate. Remove the beer jelly with mint from the mold, then put in on the salsa.

# BARLEY WINE ICE CREAM AND BARLEY MALT ICE CREAM WITH LIME

### SERVES 4

FOR THE BEER ICE CREAM
14 OZ (400 G) CREAM
3/4 CUP+2 TBSP (200 ML)) MILK
1 1/2 CUPS (300 G) SUGAR
3 1/2 OZ (100 G) GLUCOSE
1 1/4 CUPS (300 ML) BARLEY WINE
1 LIME, VERY GREEN

FOR THE MALT ICE CREAM
10 1/2 OZ (300 G) FRESH CREAM
1 1/4 CUPS (300 ML) FRESH WHOLE MILK
1 CUP (200 G) SUGAR
2 OZ (50 G) WILDFLOWER HONEY
5 1/4 OZ (150 G) BARLEY MALT

**PREPARATION**

For the Barley Wine ice cream, boil the beer with the sugar and the glucose until it has reduced by half. Add the beer to the milk and heat to 185 °F (85 °C). Add the cream to the milk and leave to cool in the refrigerator. Then put the ice cream base in the ice cream machine and bring it to the correct consistency and a temperature of 43 to 18 °F (-6 to -8 °C).

For the malt ice cream, bring the milk to 185 °F (85 °C) with the sugar, the malt and the honey, mixing it with a whisk. Leave to become tepid and then add the fresh cream. Let it cool thoroughly and put it in the ice cream machine to whisk until it reaches the correct consistency.

Serve in a small bowl and grate the fresh lime zest over it. If you add a few edible flowers such as violets, this will give a final touch to the finished dish.

PAIRING BEER AND FOOD

# BOCK FOAM,
# CANDIED FRUIT AND
# SWEET FRIED PASTRY CASSATA STYLE

SERVES 4

**FOR THE BEER FOAM**
3/4 CUP+2 TBSP (200 ML)) BOCK
4 LEAVES GELATIN
2 OZ (50 G) BARLEY MALT
2 OZ (50 G) ACACIA HONEY
1/2 CUP (100 G) SUGAR

**FOR THE FILLING**
7 OZ (200 G) FRESH COW'S MILK RICOTTA
3 OZ (80 G) ACACIA HONEY

**FOR THE SWEET FRIED PASTRY**
3 CUPS (400 G) FLOUR
1/3 CUP (80 G) BUTTER
2 OZ (50 G) GRANULATED SUGAR
2 EGGS
1 EGG WHITE
1/3 OZ (10 G) BITTER CHOCOLATE
2 OZ (50 G) MARSALA
4 TSP (40 ML) WHITE WINE VINEGAR
4 CUPS (1 LITER) CORN OIL FOR FRYING
7 OZ (200 G) MIXED CANDIED FRUIT

**PREPARATION**

For the pastry, combine the sugar and butter with an electric whisk to make a foamy mixture. Add one egg at a time and then the egg whites, the bitter chocolate and the flour, mixing all the ingredients thoroughly, then pour in the vinegar and the Marsala. Roll out the mixture into sheets about 1/16 in (1.5 millimeters) thick. Using a round cookie cutter, cut out discs and roll them round metal cannoli tubes, then fry them for 1 minute in the corn oil previously brought up to temperature. Drain, leave to cool and slide them off the cylinders.

Cut the candied fruit into small dice and put them in a container in the refrigerator.

For the beer foam, soften the gelatin in cold water. Bring the beer to the boil with the sugar, honey and barley malt, then wring out the gelatin and dissolve it in the beer. Mix it well with a whisk and put the mixture in a siphon with 1 nitrogen cartridge. Let it rest in the refrigerator for at least one hour.

Stir together the cold ricotta and the honey, mixing it well and put it in the refrigerator.
Remove the siphon from the refrigerator, shake it and fill the two ends of the cannoli, one with the foam and the other with the ricotta-honey mixture. Finally sprinkle with the diced candied fruits to decorate.

# GLOSSARY

ACETIC: A descriptor for aromatic beers with hints and nuances reminiscent of vinegar. Positive and desirable in some cases (in sour beers or matured in barrels) but unacceptable in all others.

ALCOHOL: One of the products of fermentation.

ALE: Top-fermented beer.

ALFA ACIDS: These are expressed numerically and together they represent the bitter substances in hops. The higher the value, the greater the bittering power of the hops.

AMILASES (ALFA AND BETA): The enzymes that in mashing break down the long chains of complex starch sugars into simple sugars.

BARLEY: The cereal that, once it has been malted, is the main ingredient of beer.

BARLEY MALT: Barley that has undergone the malting process.

BEER: Generic term for any type of beer.

BODY: A characteristic of the finished beer, and more particularly an element of gustatory evaluation. It ranges from "watery" to "viscous" and it depends on the unfermented residual sugar (dextrine) and other substances.

BOILING: The phase of the production process in which the wort is boiled and the hops are added.

BREWING: The whole "hot" process in which the wort is created that will be fermented after it has cooled.

BREW PUB: A pub that produces its own beer that it offers to its clients but does not sell commercially outside.

CARBON DIOXIDE, $CO_2$: Gas produced by yeast during fermentation and secondary fermentation in bottle.

CEREALS: Plants whose fruits or seeds are rich in starch and are therefore used for fermenting.

COLOR (of beer): This may be derived exclusively from the types of malts used or, in some cases, by special ingredients added, such as fruit for example.

DIACETYL: A molecule produced during fermentation that provides "buttery" notes. In some ales it is acceptable at low levels but it is not welcome in lagers.

DMS: Dimethyl sulfide, an aromatic molecule reminiscent of boiled corn. It is almost always a defect.

DRY-HOPPING: A flavoring technique that consists of adding hops to the fermentaion vessel after fermentation has finished, or into barrels.

ESTERS: Agreeable aromatic compounds in the "fruity" category. They arise from the combination and reaction of various substances in the production process (in particular yeast and alcohol, depending on the fermentation temperature).

FERMENTATION: The process by which yeast converts the wort into beer. The sugars are metabolized by the yeast that mainly produces alcohol and carbon dioxide, as well as numerous by-products.

FILTRATION: Phase of the preparation of beer in which the mash liquid is separated from the solid parts of the cereal grains (spent grains).

GERMINATION: An important stage of malting in which the seeds of the cereal are allowed to germinate to activate their enzymatic potential.

GRUIT (OR GRUYT): A collection of herbs, leaves, roots and various essences that until the 17th century was used for bittering and flavoring beer before the introduction of hops.

HOP: A dioecious perennial climber that can reach a height of 20 to 26 feet (6 to 8 meters). The female flowers are rich in resinous substances and essential oils and they are used to give the beer its bitter taste and enrich its aromas.

IBU (International Bitterness Unit): The measure of bitterness derived from hops.

IMPERIAL: An adjective generally used to emphasize a more "rich and powerful" version of a certain style. For example, Imperial IPA, Imperial Stout, Imperial Pils etc.

LAGER: Bottom-fermented beer.

LAMBIC: A spontaneously fermented beer characteristic of Belgium, that is sour, complex and suitable for ageing.

LUPULIN: The aromatic oils and resins of hops.

MALTING: The process by which cereal grains are soaked, germinated and then dried or caramelized or toasted.

MASHING: The preparatory phase of beer making during which the sugary wort is produced. A mixture of water and malted milled cereals is "brewed" at a particular temperature to activate the enzymes.

OXIDATION: The set of chemical reactions caused by the presence of an excess of oxygen in the finished beer or simply the result of ageing or poor storage. Oxidised beer has the smell of wet cardboard.

PASTEURIZATION: The thermal process that beer may undergo to eliminate any micro-organisms. It is widespread among large indurstial brewers but frowned on by small micro-breweries.

PHENOLS: Family of aromatic phenolic compounds with fragrances ranging from medicinal to smoky, from cloves to tar.

RAW: An ambiguous term. It indicates an unpasteurized beer, but the beer is still produced by brewing the malted grain.

REINHEITSGEBOT: The Purity Law of beer. Dating from 1516 in Bavaria, it decreed that beers might only be made with water, malted barley and hops (yeast had not yet been discovered).

SPARGING: The process of rinsing cereal grains with warm water to extract all the simple sugars produced.

SPENT GRAIN: The solid, insoluble part of the mashed cereal that must be removed before boiling.

STYLE (of beer): The objective and measurable data that defines a particular type of beer

YEAST: A single-celled organism of the *Saccharomyces* family that is responsible for the fermentation of the beer and therefore for the alcohol and carbon dioxide present in it.

**FABIO PETRONI** was born in Corinaldo, Ancona, in 1964. Currently he lives and works in Milan. After studying photography, he has worked with some of the most celebrated professionals in the field. His career has led him to specialize in portraits and still life, areas in which he has demonstrated an intuitive, precise style. Over the years he has photographed people well-known in the fields of culture, medicine and the Italian economy. He works with the main advertising agencies and has been responsible for many campaigns for important international clients and businesses. For White Star Publishers he has published *Horses: Master Portraits* (2010), *Mutt's Life!* (2011), *Cocktails, Roses* and *Super Cats* (2012), *Orchids, Tea Sommelier, Chili Pepper: Moments of Spicy Passion* (2013), and *Bonsai* (2014). He is the official photographer of the IJRC (International Jumping Riders Club) and is responsible for the visual side of its publicity devoted to international equestrian competitions. www.fabiopetronistudio.com

**PETER FONTANA**, vintage 1971 from the region of Brianza. Married to Federica (a non-drinker!), they have three children: Arturo (in honor of the great brewing entrepreneur Arthur Guinness), Paolo and Caterina. He got into beer in adolescence in provocative opposition to his friends who only drank wine. In 1990, the night before his final exams, he was nagged with doubts about his future as he sat in a nondescript pub in front of a bottle of Trompe-la-Mort that he had never seen or drunk before. At that moment he made a decision that would change his life: to collect beer bottles, empty ones because they had been drunk.
Italy at that time offered little in this line, but the boundaries opened up as he traveled through Europe in his university years: Germany, Belgium, England and Ireland were a bottomless pit from which to draw. The space he had in his room to collect 100 bottles quickly filled up, and the discovery of completely new tastes and flavors fascinated him so much that his curiosity grew more and more.
In 1996, when the first artisanal micro-breweries opened in Italy, he was there to enjoy them, but mostly to collect the bottles. His bedroom has now been invaded by more than 2,000 bottles that are all neatly displayed in special bottle racks with cupboards above. As the collection grows, he has sadly had resort to boxes stacked in a cellar for storing the empty bottles. But as the passion for collecting seemed a bit silly, he then sought other intersts elsewhere.
He played the role of Borgrem the cleric during long nights playing Dungeons & Dragons with friends. Then at some point in the game he acquired an abbey and began a brewery to support the inhabitants of his village: a seed has been planted. It would flower a little later, in London in 1999, with a revelation: they sold kits to make beer at home. He returned from England with the plastic fermenter inside his suitcase and his dirty clothes inside the fermenter. It was time to make beer on his own!
He studied the many Americans websites about making beer at home: in the United States home brewing was already widespread. He modified a hand pasta machine to turn it into a little grain mill; he made the small amount of equipment needed and he acquired the necessary large saucepans. He put the can of malt extract supplied with the kit from London to one side. Then with his friends he started to brew beer from raw materials: malted barley grains, hop flowers and yeast. An English Strong Ale with 8% alcohol. It was love at first sight!
From then on, every month he has tried something different, with new ingredients and new styles, involving friends and presenting the results at the first competitions for Italian home brewers. There comparisons can be made, and the will to do even better grows.
In 2008 he started the craft micro-brewery in Monza of which he still the owner and brewer: the *Piccolo Opificio Brassicolo del Carrobiolo - FERMENTUM*, a member of the Italian Union Birrai. As well as producing sought-after beers, using local ingredients and special recipes, he organizes introductory courses for home production and for tasting of quality beers. His beers and his brewery have won the highest awards in the last three editions of the *Guida alle Birre d'Italia*, published by Slow Food Editore.
In 2014 the brewery was expanded with a new production facility, adding a brew pub (the first in his city) to enable the many enthusiasts to sample its beers in the proper manner.

**JOHN RUGGIERI**, was born in Bethlehem in 1984 but grew up in Piedmont. He has trained professionally in many "starred" kitchens, such as those of the *Piazza Duomo* in Alba and the *Scrigno del Duomo* in Trento. Now chef of the *Refettorio Simplicitas*, a restaurant of polished elegance in the heart of the Brera district of Milan, Ruggieri is devoted to spreading a newly rediscovered approach to food based on simplicity, with a strong emphasis on the quality of raw materials: these are selected on the basis of seasonality and authenticity. Ruggieri's dishes and flavors follow the most authentic traditions, using anew many of the niche products to be found in his region. His is a simple style of cuisine, sober, balanced and, in its way, almost ascetic.

**ANDREA CAMASCHELLA**, editor and author of *Fermento Birra Magazine* and co-ordinator of the *Guida alle Birre d'Italia* published by Slow Food Editore, is a professor and judge in brewing competitions.

# ALPHABETICAL INDEX OF STYLES

# ALPHABETICAL INDEX OF NAMES

# ALPHABETICAL INDEX OF RECIPE INGREDIENTS

## PHOTO CREDITS

The authors would like to thank:

Andrea Camaschella and Michele Di Paola for monitoring the text.

Birra del Carrobiolo - P.O.B.C. Fermentum di Monza - for the beers and materials they made available.
Sherwood Pub of Nicorvo (Pavia, Italy) - Bere Buona Birra and Lambic Zoon of Milan for the props.

WHITE STAR PUBLISHERS

WS White Star Publishers® is a registered trademark owned
by De Agostini Libri S.p.A.

© 2014 De Agostini Libri S.p.A.
Via G. da Verrazano, 15 - 28100 Novara, Italy
www.whitestar.it - www.deagostini.it

Translation and editing: Rosetta Translations SARL

ISBN 978-88-544-0901-9
1 2 3 4 5 6   18 17 16 15 14

Printed in China